LOW CARB,
HEALTHY FAT

This book is proudly dedicated to all the people who have been given poor or misleading information about carbs and fat. I cannot wait for the day that the correct information is taught in schools – then we will see a health revolution for the coming generations.

Cook with love and laughter!
Pete xo

LOW CARB, HEALTHY FAT

The simplest way to ACHIEVE + MAINTAIN a HEALTHY WEIGHT

With more than 130 LOW-CARB, KETO-FRIENDLY recipes

PETE EVANS

 plum.  Pan Macmillan Australia

A NOTE FROM THE AUTHOR

This book is about how a diet low in carbohydrates and including healthy fats can improve overall good health. It explains some of the emerging science showing the positive effects of a low-carb, healthy-fat diet and some of the medical problems that may stem from or are associated with a diet high in processed carbs and lacking in good fats. It is important to note that much of this science is in its early stages, though I have endeavoured to provide references to some of the best studies that are available at this point in time (see Further Reading, page 302). I believe that a good diet of unprocessed food that is low in carbs and includes healthy fats and a moderate amount of protein (in other words, a paleo diet) is one of the best ways to improve your overall health. These opinions are based on my own experiences and those of the thousands of people who write to me about their diet via social media. Nutritional science is constantly evolving. For example, less than a decade ago many doctors were urging us to eat more carbs and less fat; now the message is reversed. It is my hope and expectation that the principles of the paleo diet will soon be mainstream and the subject of numerous studies. I am not saying that a paleo diet is a cure for disease or presenting the paleo diet as gold-standard science at this stage; but I am saying it is an excellent plan for avoiding some of the ingredients that have a demonstrated negative effect on our health, and incorporating ingredients with proven benefits.

CONTENTS

INTRODUCTION

I believe it's more important than ever for us to know how to support our own health and wellbeing. That's why I'm stoked to bring you *Low Carb, Healthy Fat,* which is full of all the information, tips, tricks and recipes you need to make food your medicine.

In the following pages, I'll share the reasons why adopting a low-carbohydrate way of eating is one of the best things we can do to live long, healthy lives. By reducing sugar- and starch-based carbohydrates in our meals and instead combining in-season vegetables with a moderate amount of high-quality protein, enough healthy fat to satiate and some fermented foods, we can quickly and easily unlock our body's natural potential for fast, healthy weight loss, improve our mood and energy levels and support better brain function.

I've personally experienced the awesome benefits of taking a low-carb approach, and now the latest nutritional research is indicating that this way of living appears to offer some protection from chronic diseases, especially the metabolic conditions that are currently reaching epidemic proportions. This has inspired me to create a simple action plan; a way to help you take achievable steps towards making sustainable health your number-one priority.

If you have turned to this book for help with weight loss, I must ask you to change your perspective. You see, weight is not a true indicator of health. Yet one of the lovely side effects of reducing carbohydrates and replacing them with veggies, proteins and healthy fats is that your weight will normalise, so you can lose the additional kilos that may have been hindering your adventures in life. Or, if you have been underweight or malnourished for some time, you might actually gain a little until you reach a healthy weight. I also need to advise you that nobody can claim to have all the answers when it comes to weight control. Because weight is so variable and multi-factorial, there's no 'one-size-fits-all' approach.

Ultimately, what this is about is examining the many factors that come into play when we look to adopt a sustainable, healthy lifestyle long-term. Yes, this is a *lifestyle*. Not a diet. It's your chance to support your health, wellbeing and longevity through the foods and drinks you choose, the length and quality of your sleep, your level of activity, and the power of living mindfully. We'll also investigate how to offset the impact of environmental toxins and external and internal stresses through the way you cook, eat, rest and exercise.

As many of you will be aware, I, along with many others, promote a paleo way of life. This basically means I try to eat and live in a similar way to the earliest humans. No, it's not based on chowing down like cavemen! Instead, the concept is about taking basic principles from what we know of the Palaeolithic Era – as well as from contemporary hunter–gatherer communities – and combining these with aspects of the most current scientific research.

What can we learn about diet and lifestyle when we look to our palaeolithic ancestors and modern hunter–gatherer communities? All the evidence we have indicates that our hunter–gatherer and paleo ancestors were fit, lean and muscular, obviously with no need to join a gym or follow government nutritional guidelines backed by large-scale agriculture and multinational corporations. Nor did they have to interpret the confusing food pyramids that exist today. Instead, everything was organic, wild-caught, seasonal and delicious ... just as nature intended! Nor was their food manipulated, genetically modified, dosed with artificial fertilisers or tainted by pesticides.

By contrast, our modern bodies have no idea what to do with the food many of us eat today except to manifest dis-ease. We are simply consuming too many insulin-spiking foods, in the form of carbohydrates, which are actively promoted by many of our health authorities. Our digestion has not evolved to cope with the processed, carbohydrate-rich 'Frankenfoods' that now fill our every waking minute. Advertised on TV, radio, social media and billboards, these highly refined, unnatural foods are everywhere: on the internet, in petrol stations, supermarkets and corner shops, even in our kids' schools. We can't escape them. Taking into account that the typical Australian diet derives 45 per cent of its calorific intake from carbs, and the fact that 60–70 per cent of us are overweight, clearly we've taken a pretty hefty wrong turn somewhere along the way.

OUR DIGESTION HAS NOT EVOLVED TO COPE WITH THE PROCESSED, CARBOHYDRATE-RICH 'FRANKENFOODS' THAT NOW FILL OUR EVERY WAKING MINUTE

Of course, the amount of carbohydrates we eat has a direct (and massive) effect on our blood-sugar – or more accurately, our blood-glucose – levels, because all carbohydrates are broken down into sugars in the body and released into the bloodstream as glucose. The basic rule of thumb: the higher the total carbohydrate content, and the more refined and highly processed these carbohydrates, the more rapidly they will increase blood-sugar levels.

Compare our current 'carbovore' ways to those of our palaeolithic ancestors, and of hunter–gatherer communities today. They rely on vegetables, a moderate amount of protein and plenty of good fat, their metabolisms fine-tuned to take advantage when 'the hunting is good'. In fact, in nature, there is no such thing as an obese or overweight wild animal, because they instinctively eat to survive, eating well when food is plentiful and storing energy for times when the hunting, foraging or grazing is scarce. We humans (because, after all, we are animals too) also developed survival mechanisms for when hunting and gathering weren't plentiful, including the ability of our bodies to run on either glucose or fat for energy.

This simple observation can help us to understand how our bodies work best. Basically, by significantly reducing the amount of carbohydrates we eat and increasing our intake of vegetables, good-quality protein and healthy fats, we can increase the body's natural capacity to burn fat (in much the same way our ancestors did). When we move into this fat-burning state – which is called ketosis – we teach our body to burn its own fat as an energy source, rather than the carbohydrates (as glucose) from our latest meal. In ketosis, the liver breaks the fat down into fatty acids and ketones, and our cells use the ketones

LOW-CARB, HEALTHY-FAT VERSUS TYPICAL AUSTRALIAN DIET

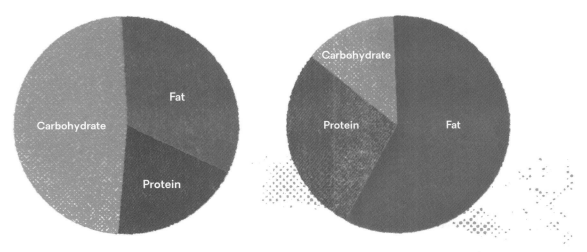

Typical Australian diet   **Low-carb, healthy-fat diet**

rather than glucose as a fuel source. And when our bodies utilise energy from these slow-burning units of fat – known as ketones – we tend to feel less hungry.

Recent Australian research also confirms that following a low-carb diet has long-lasting effects in significantly stabilising blood-glucose levels and protecting against the onset and development of metabolic diseases. However, the study finds that there is no current evidence to prove that a low-carb diet triggers an increase in the production of ketones from fat deposits. It also concludes that it remains unclear from current research how great the carbohydrate restriction must be before ketosis kicks in. While a traditional low-carb diet may include 50–100 grams of carbs per day, a ketogenic (KETO) approach aims for less than 50 grams and ideally closer to 20 grams per day. I personally follow a mild ketogenic approach, without measuring out how many grams of carbs I am eating. If you would like to measure out the total grams of carbs you are going to consume per day, then feel free to do so, as you may enjoy the process; or you can simply follow the meal plans and recipes in this book or adapt your own favourite recipes to be low carb or ketogenic. (Please note that the desserts in this book are not all ketogenic as they contain honey.)

To help you get your head around it all, I want to share two analogies to explain how we might best fuel our bodies in a way that supports optimal health and longevity.

My dear friend and mentor Nora Gedgaudas explains this beautifully when she talks about fuelling our metabolic fireplace. We all have a metabolic fireplace within us that produces energy. Now, for most of the western population, whose diet is based on 70 per cent carbohydrates, it's like keeping your metabolic fire burning by having to continually add kindling, as such small pieces of wood burn fast and then the fire quickly dies down again. For anyone eating a western-style diet that consists of bread or cereal for breakfast, a mid-morning snack, a sandwich, roll, wrap or sushi for lunch, another afternoon snack to get through the last few hours of the day, and then pasta, rice or pizza for dinner, this is – nutritionally speaking – the same as keeping a fire going with kindling. And it's exhausting for our bodies, because it takes us on a blood-sugar roller-coaster every single day.

Yet there is a completely different way we can choose to fuel our metabolic fire: one that doesn't cause insulin spikes, food cravings or the need to constantly refuel. By simply placing a fat log on the fire between one and three times a day (depending on our circumstances), we can lengthen the time it takes to survive on the fuel from each meal.

The second analogy involves a petrol tanker: imagine a petrol tanker. It has its own petrol tank, which powers the main truck carrying the huge tank full of petrol on its trailer, but it can't access the vast reserves of petrol it is hauling because it isn't engineered that way – at most it can access the few hundred litres or so in its fuel tank. And this is how our bodies work when we use glucose as our primary source of fuel. It's also why endurance athletes believe they need to 'carb up', because they run their small fuel tank down in a similar way. But when you adapt to burning fat as your primary source of fuel, you can access a virtually limitless supply of energy from your fat stores. It's basically like the truck being able to tap into the huge petrol tank on its trailer, without having to stop every thousand kilometres to refuel.

EATING THE FOODS OUR ANCESTORS THRIVED ON IS A SURE-FIRE WAY WE CAN HELP OURSELVES BE HEALTHIER

For all these reasons, eating the foods our ancestors thrived on is a sure-fire way we can help ourselves be healthier. While it won't necessarily heal or cure all of our ills, I reckon giving your body the 'fuel' (that is, nutrients) it desperately needs is a bloody good place to start. And from a nutritional and scientific standpoint, a low-carbohydrate approach is the best way to set yourself on the path to regaining your health and managing weight issues. The human body might be an incredibly complex system, but the way we fuel it doesn't have to be: if we choose to use the fuel nature intended – which is fat – suddenly all the pieces fall into place. The food we get to eat is also scrumptious! Real, healthy wholefoods from the purest, sustainable and most ethical sources we can find.

Once you start to train your body and brain to fuel themselves with healthy fats, your brain knows 'the hunting is good' and that it doesn't need to cling to excess stores of fat. What happens instead? You start to burn fat as energy. By doing this, we can basically 'turn off' the emotional, carb-craving monster that we may have become and instead 'turn on' our body's natural ability to be clean, lean and resistant to disease. I reckon it's time we realised that this is a healthier option – for ourselves and the planet.

Over the following pages, we'll cover what to eat to fuel your body best, how to sleep and rest effectively, how to get your body moving daily and how to use breathing to calm your nervous system and live mindfully. A simple meal plan will help you to easily make the changes you need to and stick to them ... for good. Finally, I have provided more than 130 delicious low-carb recipes, covering snacks, soups, meals, sides, treats, drinks and basics.

But first, a gentle reminder: it's important to listen to your body every step of the way. Everyone is an individual, and as we all have different needs, it's advisable to consult your healthcare professional so you have their support during this journey. For example, pregnant women, breastfeeding women and children have higher protein requirements than the rest of us, so a moderate-protein approach will not be suitable. If you have an existing medical condition, always discuss any changes you plan to make to your diet and lifestyle with your doctor and make sure your health is carefully monitored through this transition and beyond.

Getting rid of sugar, junk foods and caffeine from your diet can initially leave you feeling worse. Some people experience flu-like symptoms or withdrawal reactions, including fatigue and headaches, emotional or cognitive symptoms, feelings of queasiness and short-term digestive discomfort. Be sure to drink plenty of fresh, purified water – but I like to avoid drinking it with meals, as I believe it can interfere with digestion.

You may also wish to take supplements of key vitamins and minerals, as these can be more difficult to obtain even through natural food sources these days. Be aware that you may experience some temporary health effects when you dramatically cut your carb intake. These can include headaches, bad breath, weakness, fatigue, constipation and diarrhoea. As always, if symptoms are troublesome or persistent, consult your healthcare professional.

With those caveats out the way, I invite you to come with me on this journey – there's really nothing scary or complicated here. After all, I'm no scientist. I'm simply a chef who passionately shares what information I've learned about how we can regain better health. If you want to learn more about any of this, go to the 'Further reading' section on page 302, as there are whole books written on these subjects. My goal here is to help you understand the basics and encourage you to create delicious meals for yourself and your family. And because I'd prefer that you were in the kitchen rather than reading about it, it's time to get started.

Cook with love and laughter,

Pete Evans

PART one

WHY a LOW-CARB, HEALTHY-FAT DIET?

EATING THE LOW-CARB, HEALTHY-FAT WAY

How we look and feel, and whether or not the cells of our body stay healthy, begins with what we choose to eat. From the way certain foods affect our hormones to which vegetables are best to help protect and detoxify, I want to show you as clearly as possible what I think we should eat and not eat, so you can enjoy all the health benefits of a low-carb, healthy fat lifestyle.

MACRONUTRIENTS: THE BIG PICTURE

The food we eat provides us with three macronutrients: fat, protein and carbohydrates. Our bodies use the essential fatty acids from fat as a booster for our skin, heart, brain and all our other vital organs, while proteins supply essential amino acids, which are important for building and maintaining the structure of our bodies and helping to regulate its processes. Together with micronutrients (vitamins and minerals), these play a crucial role in helping us to live long, healthy and happy lives.

In today's modern world, we are bombarded with highly processed carbohydrate foods that contain a significant amount of sugar and starch. Yet our bodies have no need for these carbohydrates, and they can damage our health. Instead, it's about choosing carbohydrate foods that are the 'good guys' – foods such as leafy greens and fibrous vegetables. These are the ones that offer clear benefits and no real downsides. While our brains do need some glucose (sugar) – for example when we need to exert lots of energy in an emergency – we don't want to run predominantly on this fuel source. Instead, by pairing sensible low-carb options with healthy fats, we are able to eat in a way that keeps our blood-sugar and insulin levels low.

The latest scientific research suggests that the food we eat is a powerful tool when it comes to our health. That's why, in this book, I'll show you how to shift your ratio of macronutrients in a healthier direction, reduce the proportion of calories you get from unhelpful carbohydrates and replace them with seasonal veggies, low-sugar fruits and some fermented veggies, a moderate amount of protein from sustainable sources and, of course, healthy fats.

FOODS TO EMBRACE

Fewer carbs

More carbs

Coconut oil, nuts & animal fat

Fish & seafood

Meat

Eggs

Vegetables

FOODS TO AVOID OR REDUCE

Fewer carbs   **More carbs**

High-sugar fruit

Potatoes

Beer

Pasta, cooked

Rice, cooked

Bread

Soft drink

Doughnut

Chocolate bar

Lollies

GLUCOSE AND INSULIN: WHAT YOU NEED TO KNOW

When we eat carbohydrate foods, our blood-glucose levels rise. In response, the pancreas releases insulin, which instructs the cells to take the glucose up as fuel or store it as glycogen in the liver. Once they do this, though, the body then stores any excess glucose as fat. When we habitually eat foods high in processed carbohydrates, our blood-glucose levels stay high or fluctuate wildly, and more and more insulin is released. This imbalance can lead to a condition called insulin resistance, where the cells cease to respond to the increased insulin levels and both insulin and blood-glucose remain high.

When insulin resistance kicks in, our bodies start to store excess body fat (particularly around our hips and stomach); it also leaves us feeling tired after meals and subject to endless food cravings, and more. Eventually this puts so much strain on the pancreas that it ceases producing insulin altogether – this is type 2 diabetes. The consistently high blood sugar is damaging for our blood vessels and the organs they supply, the cells don't get the fuel they need to function optimally, and even though excess glucose is laid down as fat, there is always more because it's not being dealt with as it should.

COMMON FOODS, HIDDEN SUGARS

The following illustration shows the amount of sugar released into the bloodstream by eating common foods, such as bread, rice and pasta.

1 portion white rice
= 13–15 teaspoons sugar

1 portion rolled oats
= 12 teaspoons sugar

1 portion brown rice
= 10 teaspoons sugar

1 portion noodles or pasta
= 9 teaspoons sugar

2 slices white bread
= 7 teaspoons sugar

2 slices wholemeal bread
= 5 teaspoons sugar

Insulin resistance is just one of many risk factors, along with high blood pressure and obesity, for stroke, heart disease and type 2 diabetes. When you have a cluster of these risk factors, you have what is called metabolic syndrome. And given that nearly two-thirds of Australian adults are overweight or obese and there are an estimated one million of us with type 2 diabetes, it's clear we need to think hard about the way we eat.

When our ancestors were roaming the earth hunting and gathering, insulin helped us lay down reserves of fat ready for times when food was scarce, such as over winter. However, if we fast-forward to today, when our supermarket shelves are groaning with sugar- and starch-based carbohydrates, we're faced with a very different equation. No longer is insulin allowing us to store fat for emergencies. Instead, the amounts of refined carbohydrates we're consuming have completely tipped our biochemical balance – and, with our blood-sugar levels surging out of control, we're basically making fat 365 days of the year.

The good news is you can stop insulin resistance in its tracks. By drastically reducing the amount of carbohydrates you eat, replacing them with good, healthy fats, exercising and managing your stress levels, you will be taking steps to reduce your blood sugar and reclaim your health.

WHERE ARE YOU STARTING FROM?

There are some basic tests we can use to help us understand where our body is at, and to track and monitor our progress while we're on the road to better health. By taking measurements every week or month, we learn more about ourselves and so are able to make better decisions about the next steps.

Our waist-to-hip ratio (WHR) acts as a marker of our insulin sensitivity. If we are able to process insulin properly, fat gets deposited evenly around our body. However, when we become insulin resistant, fat gets stored around our internal organs. This disrupts the signals sent by our hormones to tell us when we are full and when we are hungry, and makes us susceptible to poor health and disease.

To calculate your WHR, divide the circumference of your waist by the circumference of your hips. Your waist is measured at the mid-point between your bottom rib and the top of your hip bone; and your hip measurement is the greatest circumference of your behind. Compare your results to the chart below. The idea is to aim for an excellent ratio; average or less on this chart will put you at higher risk of insulin resistance and, in turn, metabolic diseases.

WAIST-TO-HIP RATIO BY GENDER

WAIST-TO-HIP RATIO (WHR) NORMS				
Gender	Excellent	Good	Average	At Risk
Male	<0.85	0.85–0.89	0.90–0.95	≥0.95
Female	<0.75	0.75–0.79	0.80–0.86	≥0.86

Once you've done your first test, take the same measurements monthly and monitor how your WHR changes as you eat low carb and pay more attention to the way you sleep, move and engage with the world.

Another important measure to understand is blood glucose. Blood-glucose levels are measured in millimoles per litre of blood (mmol/L), with normal levels falling in the range of 4.0–7.8 mmol/L. The key to effective dietary management of blood glucose is to ensure it stays within this range. Blood-glucose levels are usually tested in a 'fasting' state – when you haven't had anything to eat or drink for eight hours. The normal range for fasting blood-glucose levels is 3.0–5.5 mmol/L. By recording your findings, you can get a picture of how your blood-glucose levels respond to diet and lifestyle.

By doing regular tests of our blood-glucose levels, we can also find out if we are at risk of type 2 diabetes. You can easily do this by taking a finger-stick blood test and then checking the results using a glucose meter. Blood-glucose meters are sold as kits with everything you need. There are lots of great apps for your smartphone or computer to help you understand and track these results. Note that if you already have type 2 diabetes and you're taking medication to reduce blood glucose, you will need to make dietary changes in consultation with your doctor, to avoid a sudden hypoglycaemic episode.

Another sign of insulin resistance is elevated blood pressure (hypertension). Elevated blood pressure can cause hardening of the arteries and damage to the kidneys and heart. You can check your blood pressure by purchasing a blood-pressure monitor for home use, or by going to a doctor or pharmacy. Your blood-pressure reading is composed of two numbers: the higher number (systolic) shows the highest blood pressure in your arteries, when your heart beats; and the lower number (diastolic) is the lowest pressure in your arteries, between heartbeats.

UNDERSTANDING BLOOD-PRESSURE READINGS

BLOOD-PRESSURE CLASSIFICATION	SYSTOLIC/DIASTOLIC
Low	<90 and <60
Normal	90–120 and 60–80
Pre-hypertension	120–139 or 80–89
Stage 1 Hypertension	140–159 or 90–99
Stage 2 Hypertension	≥160 or ≥100

If your blood pressure is above the normal range, you need to take steps to sort it out.

What's interesting is that when you set your carbohydrate intake to a level that works for your body, it causes a rapid loss of water, and this works to bring blood pressure down. The other nice thing is that blood pressure is often one of the first things to improve when you implement diet and lifestyle changes, so it gives you a fairly immediate sense of progress. If you're already on blood-pressure medication you need to make lifestyle changes in close consultation with your doctor to avoid sudden low blood pressure.

If you do have high blood pressure, it is a good idea to test it weekly at first. Once it's at a healthy level, it's worth checking your blood pressure at least twice a year. Meanwhile, low blood pressure is considered to be below 90/60. Symptoms may include light-headedness, dizziness and weakness and blurry vision. If you have symptoms of low blood pressure, contact your medical professional.

LEPTIN: WHY IT'S KEY

If our metabolism is the steam engine that keeps our bodies running, our hormones act like the driver, telling us to power up or conserve energy so we can complete the whole journey. Leptin is the hormone that switches all these other hormones on and off, as well as controlling vital functions in the brain. Only discovered in 1994, leptin is one of several hormones produced by body fat, which functions as a complex endocrine organ, secreting hormones directly into the blood. Leptin basically sends signals to our brain to tell it when we are full and should stop eating, and also when we are in 'starvation mode'. As a result, the way leptin operates has a huge impact on our emotions, food cravings and behaviour.

Ensuring leptin is working efficiently in your body is important because it helps to regulate energy and suppress food intake. If this doesn't happen, erratic fluctuations in the levels of leptin (in tandem with the 'hunger' hormone ghrelin, which makes you feel hungry) affect your ability to lose weight because they disrupt the signals to your brain that tell you when you are full and when you are hungry.

WHY SHOULD I CARE ABOUT LEPTIN?

Normalising your leptin levels is one of the best ways to help kickstart your body's natural fat-burning process. Leptin resistance occurs years before insulin resistance but is caused by the same thing – high fat-storage levels in response to high blood glucose, mostly as a result of a diet high in sugar- and starch-based carbohydrates, medication and sugary drinks – and stops your 'off switch' from working correctly. If you have leptin resistance, it's likely to prompt you to eat more often and frequently, hover over the fridge and generally experience very intense food cravings. As leptin is instrumental in our immune response, leptin resistance may also make us more prone to inflammatory conditions, such as cardiovascular disease, inflammatory bowel disease and endometriosis, especially if we're overweight or obese.

SO WHAT CAN I DO TO KEEP MY LEPTIN LEVELS HEALTHY?

The good news is that leptin loves fat, so eating lots of natural fats and excluding damaging sugary foods from your diet is a great start. It's also important to give your body and mind enough time to rest, repair and recuperate. Every time you do this you are helping the receptors in your body and brain to become more sensitive to this important regulating hormone. In a nutshell, stabilising your leptin levels is one of the ways you can enjoy long-lasting energy, a focused mind and balanced moods to do the things you love – whether it's work, rest or play.

'FRANKENFOODS': PROCESSED FOODS AND HIDDEN SUGARS

Since the 1970s the amount of hidden sugars, hydrogenated oils and genetically modified organisms (GMOs) in our food has increased significantly. In fact, 90 cents of every dollar spent on food in the United States goes on buying these highly refined, nutrient-devoid Frankenfoods. The mainstream food industry has relied on sugar to help both preserve and 'bulk out' ingredients, particularly in 'low-fat' foods, meaning sugar is more abundant than ever in our food supply.

At the same time, our food sources have become less diverse. Did you know that 90 per cent of the world's food supply comes from just 17 species of plants, with wheat, corn, rice, barley, soybeans, cane sugar, sorghum, potatoes, oats and cassava topping the list? Yet most of these did not form part of our palaeolithic ancestors' diet. Instead, our paleo ancestors derived around 90 per cent of their calorific intake from the meat and fat of between 100 and 200 different species of wild animal, with small amounts of vegetables, greens, nuts and fruits in season making up the rest.

WHAT ARE THESE FOODS DOING TO MY BODY?

Processed foods contain lots of starchy carbohydrates and hidden sugars, all of which are converted to glucose (sugar) in the bloodstream. Consuming these types of foods regularly has been proven through research to cause inflammation, and first-hand experience (such as in the hard-hitting film *Super Size Me*) backs this up. It is perhaps no coincidence that while our reliance on processed food has increased substantially over the past 30 years, we have seen drastic increases in the prevalence of type 2 diabetes and cardiovascular disease, cancer, autoimmune conditions and other chronic diseases.

Processed foods are also full of damaging fats, which effectively upset our balance of omega-6 fatty acids to omega-3 fatty acids. Crucially, processed foods fill your diet with all sorts of hidden sugars your body has no need for.

WHAT IS PROCESSED FOOD PRODUCTION DOING TO OUR PLANET?

The rise of processed foods has also led to more intensive, mono-culture farming, and when one crop is grown rather than many, it places enormous pressure on the earth's resources; such intensive agriculture is partly responsible for the depletion of our soils and ecosystems. And all too often the production of processed foods is reliant on pesticides, GMOs, chemical fertilisers and feed-lot farms.

HEALTHY FATS: FILLING AND DELICIOUS

When you are following a low-carb diet, you also need to increase the amount of healthy fats you eat. Natural fats are G-O-O-D in so many ways, supplying us with an abundance of fat-soluble nutrients, such as vitamins A, D, E and K – something our modern-day diets are lacking.

My favourite healthy fats

1 **COCONUT OIL** is a near-perfect source of healthy fats, including the building blocks our bodies use to make the ketone beta-hydroxybutyric acid, one of our brain's 'superfuels', as well as the fats needed to help our immune system fight off infections.

2 **AVOCADOS** are an excellent natural source of healthy fats. They are rich in antioxidants and also help you absorb more of these nutrients from other foods. Avocados also contain fibre, which helps to make you feel full.

3 **MACADAMIA NUTS** add a wonderful creaminess to nut milks and cheeses. They're low in carbohydrates and protein, but high in healthy fatty acids, such as oleic acid and omega-9 monounsaturated fatty acids. Macadamia nuts are also very high in antioxidants and contain lots of vitamin A, vitamin B1, iron and magnesium.

4 **EGGS** are referred to as 'nature's multivitamin' for good reason. Not only do they contain lots of healthy fats and protein, but they are also a good source of vitamins A, B2, B5 and B12, plus the mineral selenium. Just make sure you eat the yolks, because they have all the fats and nutrients; the egg white is largely protein.

5 **ANIMAL FAT** is used by the body to help support the health of our nervous, immune, digestive and endocrine systems, as well as regulate our metabolism. In fact, a University of Michigan–led study shows that animal fat is a significant source of the hormone adiponectin, which plays a role in maintaining insulin sensitivity and breaking down fat, and has been linked to a decreased risk of cardiovascular disease, type 2 diabetes and obesity-associated cancers. Good animal fats include fish oil, lard (pork fat), tallow (rendered beef fat), rendered chicken fat and duck fat.

6 **EXTRA-VIRGIN OLIVE OIL** drizzled over a salad, steamed veg or meat is one of life's great pleasures. I only cook with it at low temperatures because it has a low smoke point and is susceptible to becoming rancid at high temperatures. Go for cold-pressed, organic Australian varieties because there is no heat applied or chemicals used during the extraction process (and it's always good to buy local). Olive oil is abundant in vitamins A, E and K, and a great source of amino acids, iron, calcium, magnesium and potassium and key phytonutrients.

NOTE: If you do choose to include dairy-based fats, then ghee is the best option, as the dairy proteins are removed in ghee so people who are intolerant can still enjoy it. Ghee contains short-chain fatty acids, such as butyric acid and conjugated linoleic acid (CLA). It is also rich in fat-soluble vitamins A, E and K.

WHY DO I NEED TO KNOW WHERE THE ANIMALS I EAT COME FROM?

When you do eat meat, choose sustainable wild game or livestock that has been raised outside in the sunshine and has eaten only fresh grass, as pasture-raised animals are less likely to harbour pathogens, including the potentially deadly acid-resistant E. coli. When purchasing seafood (or if you're lucky enough to catch your own), always seek out wild-caught fin fish and prawns, and make sure any farmed oysters, mussels or other molluscs come from a clean environment.

WHY ARE HEALTHY FATS SO IMPORTANT TO EAT?

Our cells – in particular those of our hearts and brains – thrive on fat. When we eat it in its healthiest forms (and in the absence of unhealthy carbohydrates), fat becomes a source of fuel designed to nurture us in body, mind and soul. On a structural level, fats form the building blocks of our cell membranes and help us to absorb enough of the fat-soluble vitamins (A, D, E and K) from our food. They also help us maintain a natural, healthy weight by slowing down the rate at which digested food leaves the stomach (which in turn helps keep blood-sugar levels steady) and providing the creamy mouth-feel that gives us pleasure when we eat, which also assists in appetite control.

HOW CAN HEALTHY FATS HELP ME LOSE WEIGHT?

If you want to lose weight, healthy fats can help to reset your metabolism. Instead of burning only sugar, you will be activating your body's natural ability to shed fat and gain muscle mass. When you allow your fat-burning 'switch' to stay on continuously (ketosis), you can enjoy increased energy, better sleep, weight loss and a sharper brain. And the best bit? It's not even that hard!

Five tips for becoming a fat burner

1 Remember that for most people, engaging an effective and well-adapted fat-burning metabolism takes 3–6 weeks.

2 Simply eat good, healthy fats, moderate amounts of high-quality protein from sustainable land and sea sources, nuts, seeds, non-starchy vegetables, including some fermented veggies, and low-sugar seasonal fruit.

3 Remove all added sugar from your diet, and limit the amount of natural sugars you eat – this effectively 'switches on' your ability to burn fat. Be aware that when sugar and fats continue to be eaten together, the results are very different, so sugar elimination is essential.

4 Cut out all processed foods and those that contain hidden sugars.

5 Choose organic, local and seasonal, wherever possible.

FATS TO AVOID: THE BAD GUYS

It's important to understand that not all fats are created equal. The simple rule of thumb: natural fat is good, processed fat is not. These highly processed fats are commonly polyunsaturated vegetable oils, which we want to avoid. The reason for this is that the crops used for oil production are quite likely to be genetically modified, and to have been grown using chemical fertilisers and pesticides; the oil is then extracted using high heat, which can make it more prone to oxidation, or in other words rancidity.

What's more, these fats contain lots of omega-6 fatty acids. While it's important to get some omega-6s from our food sources, we've tipped the balance way out of whack. In the western world today, the average ratio of omega-6 to omega-3 fatty acids in our diet is 6:1, yet the ideal ratio is a perfectly balanced 1:1. With scientific research revealing the vital role an adequate intake of omega-3s plays in determining our health and longevity, it's important to know which fats to avoid and which fats to wholeheartedly embrace.

VERY GOOD VEGGIES: YOUR STAPLE INGREDIENTS

Greens and other vegetables grown above the ground are high in fibre, contain very little sugar or starch and are full of antioxidants and phytonutrients (plant nutrients). These are the kind of carbs we need to fuel our bodies with, because they give a slow, sustained energy release, leaving us feeling fuller for longer. There are also some very good veggies that grow below the ground too, such as carrots, radishes, leeks, onions and pumpkin. Radishes are a bitter veggie good for digestion, while leeks (plus garlic and onions)

have sulfur-containing antioxidant compounds such as allicin that help protect the body from oxidation due to free-radicals. By choosing fresh, organic vegetables (or better still, growing your own) you are selecting produce that is higher in nutrients while minimising your exposure to GMOs and pesticides. I try to eat a variety of organic or spray-free, in-season vegetables daily, with an emphasis on leafy greens such as silverbeet, spinach, chard and broccoli – and also some different coloured vegetables as well.

CARBS IN VEGGIES AT A GLANCE

Fewer carbs   **More carbs**

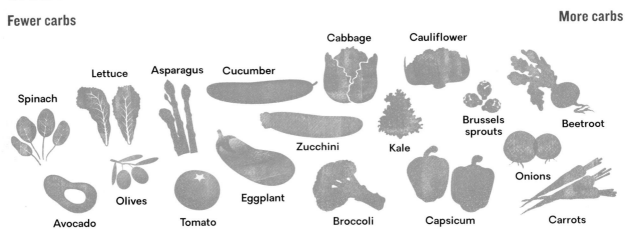

Spinach · Lettuce · Asparagus · Cucumber · Cabbage · Cauliflower · Zucchini · Kale · Brussels sprouts · Beetroot · Olives · Avocado · Tomato · Eggplant · Broccoli · Capsicum · Onions · Carrots

VEGGIES TO ENJOY			
ARTICHOKES	CAULIFLOWER	KOHLRABI	SHALLOTS
ASPARAGUS	CELERY	LEEKS	SILVERBEET
BEETROOT	CHILLIES	LETTUCE	SNOW PEAS
BOK CHOY	CHOY SUM	MUSTARD GREENS	SPINACH
BROCCOLI	CUCUMBER	ONIONS	SPRING ONIONS
BROCCOLINI	EGGPLANT	PARSLEY	SPROUTS
BRUSSELS SPROUTS	FENNEL	PUMPKIN	TOMATOES
CABBAGE	GARLIC	RADISHES	WATERCRESS
CAPSICUMS	GREEN BEANS	RHUBARB	
CARROTS	KALE	ROCKET	

NOT-SO-GOOD VEGGIES: TREAD WITH CAUTION

When following a low-carb lifestyle, there are a few vegetables that shouldn't really feature on your plate. Or if they do, only very occasionally. Starchy vegetables include roots, bulbs and kernels. While they can have some health benefits, the high starch content of these vegetables is rapidly converted to sugar in the bloodstream, which is why eating them can often cause insulin spikes, weight gain and other issues. It depends on the vegetable. Sweet potatoes, for example, can be eaten sometimes but not often, whereas potatoes are particularly problematic because they rapidly convert to glucose and are a very fast-burning source of energy. Meaning you'll just as soon crash. The problem is compounded if these vegetables are non-organic, as often the crops will have been sprayed with pesticides and fertilisers to increase yields. Some commercially grown mono-culture crops, such as corn, can be GMOs unless they are certified organic. Look for labels such as Australian Certified Organic and USDA Organic.

My advice when it comes to not-so-good vegetables? Make an informed choice that's best for you and your body and don't overdo it.

VEGGIES TO LIMIT
CORN
PARSNIPS
PEAS
POTATOES (OMIT IF POSSIBLE)
SWEET POTATOES
YAMS

FRUIT: LOW-SUGAR TREATS

When it comes to reducing your sugar intake, it's important to realise how much naturally occurring sugar (fructose) there is in most fruit – this will be processed by the liver and converted into glucose for energy or glycogen or fat for storage. That's why it's a good idea to make friends with low-sugar fruit, which you can eat more regularly. Just remember to choose organic, local and seasonal wherever possible, and to make the healthiest choice for what your body needs at the time. For example, fresh berries are rich in antioxidants and low in sugar.

HIGH-SUGAR FRUIT TO LIMIT

While fresh fruit is a good source of vitamins, minerals, phytonutrients and fibre, some fruits contain more naturally occurring sugar (as fructose) than others, and it's advisable to limit your intake of these. If you already have a metabolic condition such as obesity or diabetes, then you really need to avoid all sweet fruit, in order to help keep your blood-sugar levels steady.

FRUIT TO BE FRIENDS WITH

APPLES

AVOCADO

BLACKBERRIES

BLUEBERRIES

GRAPEFRUIT

LEMONS AND LIMES

PEARS

RASPBERRIES

STRAWBERRIES

WATERMELON

FRUIT TO LIMIT OR REDUCE

CHERRIES

DRIED FRUIT

FIGS

GRAPES

HONEYDEW MELON

KIWIFRUIT

MANGO

PAPAYA

PEACHES

PINEAPPLE

PLUMS

ROCKMELON

DAIRY: TIME TO DITCH IT?

Did you know that humans are the only animals that switch to consuming milk from another species after weaning? Personally, I don't react well to dairy, and within a few weeks of ditching it, the digestive problems and skin issues that had plagued me since childhood completely disappeared. If you're eating to make sustainable health your number-one priority, there are some reasons you might want to reconsider the inclusion of dairy products in your diet (unless you can tolerate it and can also source organic dairy).

There are a couple of things in dairy that cause some of us to react – casein (protein) and lactose (sugar). Unlike lactose, which causes an intolerance, casein proteins in milk are what's responsible for a milk allergy. This protein can, in some people, activate the immune system. For those of us with a sensitivity to casein or lactose, consuming dairy products increases our chances of suffering from digestive disorders (think reflux, constipation, diarrhoea and painful wind), as well as inflammatory conditions, such as hay fever, rheumatoid arthritis and heart disease. Medical researchers are also currently investigating whether autoimmune disorders and neurological conditions such as multiple sclerosis might be influenced by the consumption of dairy products.

On a low-carb lifestyle, the whole idea is to decrease the amount of carbohydrates you consume. As full-fat milk is relatively high in carbohydrates, it may not be the best choice you can make, even if you can tolerate it well.

Due to the fillers used to ensure a longer shelf-life and greater profitability, sometimes commercial dairy products simply aren't made up of the best ingredients. There is a chance that they may contain other substances the body's immune system could react to, thereby prompting an inflammatory response.

Another reason I choose not to eat dairy products is to protect animals and support sustainable farming practices. In Australia, the average dairy cow's milk production has increased over the past three decades from 2900 litres to as high as 5700 litres. However, the concern is that this has been achieved at the expense of animal health, with repeated pregnancies, selective breeding and supplementary feeding all taking their toll.

> **WITHIN A FEW WEEKS OF DITCHING DAIRY, THE DIGESTIVE PROBLEMS AND SKIN ISSUES THAT HAD PLAGUED ME SINCE CHILDHOOD COMPLETELY DISAPPEARED**

GRAINS: WHY WE JUST DON'T NEED THEM

Grains are the seeds of grasses, and according to cardiologist Dr William Davis, the author of *Wheat Belly*, humans are digestively ill-equipped to consume any part of grass plants, including the seeds – so the trouble with grains stems from these indigestible or poorly digested proteins.

That's why when you're eating low-carb, going grain-free is important. You see, there are many reasons why they don't serve us well both nutritionally and physiologically. Here are a few of the key reasons Dr Davis draws to our attention ...

Six good reasons for eating low carb and grain free

1 A protein found in wheat, rye and barley called gliadin produces opiates when partially digested. These bind to the brain's opiate receptors and increase appetite substantially. This may trigger **addictive relationships** with foods; especially those full of highly refined carbohydrates, such as pizza and biscuits.

2 These opiates can also influence our behaviour, meaning eating too many grain-based foods may influence the onset of **mood or food-related disorders**.

3 Grains elevate blood-sugar levels dramatically due to their high levels of starch. And the more refined the carbohydrates, the faster they are likely to **raise our blood-sugar levels**.

4 Grain phytates can **hinder absorption of important minerals**, such as iron, zinc, calcium and magnesium. Many cases of unexplained iron-deficiency anaemia, for instance, have been spontaneously reversed within several weeks of eliminating grains.

5 Numerous proteins in grains are **allergenic** and so eating grains may exacerbate the development of asthma, skin rashes and gastrointestinal distress.

6 An overconsumption of grains may also lead to **hormonal disruption**.

THE TROUBLE WITH LEGUMES

Legumes are the fruits or seeds of a leguminous plant, in other words a member of the pea family. This includes chickpeas, soya beans, peas, black beans and peanuts. Legumes may be high in protein, but they are also high in carbohydrate. While they contain fibre so they don't spike insulin levels in the same way other grain-based carbs do, it can be difficult to draw all the nutrient value from them they seem to offer.

The trouble is that legumes contain many anti-nutrients, which have the same digestion-irritating properties as grains. Anti-nutrients are natural compounds found in a variety of foods – especially grains, legumes and nuts – that interfere with the absorption of vitamins, minerals and other nutrients. They can even get in the way of the digestive enzymes, which are vital for proper nutrient absorption.

Some studies have also linked legumes with impaired thyroid function. However, the main reason to lose legumes is that they contain phytates, which inhibit the body's ability to absorb essential minerals, such as magnesium, iron and zinc.

Legumes also contain lectins, which can aggravate leaky gut syndrome. Leaky gut occurs when lectins attach to and damage the gut, allowing undigested food proteins and bacteria through the protective gut lining, causing an autoimmune response in the body.

MICROBIOME: TRUST YOUR GUT

We are only just beginning to understand the vital importance of the trillions of bacteria that live on and in us, known collectively as our microbiome. The latest research is showing that the way our microbiome functions has an impact on our genes, and this is spearheading a radical shift in our thinking about disease, hygiene and health. We're learning that our microbiome helps to regulate all manner of metabolic processes and has a key role in determining how we handle sugar and carbs, how many calories are extracted from our food, and even whether we feel hungry or full.

Given that our gut represents 70 per cent of our entire immune system, choosing foods that help to support the harmonious balance of the bacteria in our gut is one way we can keep inflammation at bay. Imbalances in the gut bacteria, known as dysbiosis, may be associated with a number of diseases. For example, new studies are investigating an apparent link between the onset of Parkinson's disease and the composition of the gut microbiome.

Gut bacteria also seem to play a part in regulating our neurotransmitters, the chemicals that affect our moods. Weight regulation and brain function also appear to be influenced by our microbiome, as do type 2 diabetes, allergies and asthma. And researchers are investigating a possible link between our microbiome and the development of some cancers, as well as its role in successful treatment.

All of this means it's more important than ever to monitor and maintain the health of your microbiome through the lifestyle you lead, by following the rule of the three Cs:

- Conscious – Be conscious of the impact the foods you put on your plate have on your health.

- Choose – Seek out unprocessed foods, know where your food comes from and choose food that's grown and cultivated in the way nature intended.

- Consumption – Understand that consumption of some chemicals, such as BPA and many of the other chemicals that may be found in plastics that we're exposed to in our modern-day world, can be detrimental to our microbiome, which is why we need the food we eat to detoxify us as much as possible.

FERMENTED FOODS: BOOST YOUR MICROBIOME

The earliest evidence of the consumption of fermented foods dates back to the Neolithic era (about 10,000 BC), and fermenting is still used by every traditional culture around the world as a way of preserving food and making it more nutritious. Having been a part of the human diet for tens of thousands of years, fermented foods are a tried-and-tested way to provide the body with beneficial bacteria and enzymes. They are loaded with vitamins and minerals, and eating just a few spoonfuls a day can help your gut to absorb as many nutrients as possible from your food.

Some of my favourite fermented foods are sauer-kraut, kimchi, coconut yoghurt and homemade

FERMENTED FOODS ARE A TRIED-AND-TESTED WAY TO PROVIDE THE BODY WITH BENEFICIAL BACTERIA AND ENZYMES

fermented sauces and condiments, such as mustard. Including a wide variety of these in our daily diet directly supplies our digestive tract with the living cultures it needs to break down the food we eat and assimilate nutrients. Fermented foods can also improve the balance of bacteria in our microbiome – this strengthens our immune system and offers us some protection against environmental pollution. Getting the delicate balance of gut bacteria right is especially important for pregnant women, as much of the mother's microbiome is passed on to her baby.

PROBIOTICS AND PREBIOTICS: POWERFUL GAME-CHANGERS

Probiotics work by creating the right conditions for healthy gut bacteria to flourish. Scientific studies have proven that probiotics support our wellbeing by preventing the overgrowth of pathogens (disease-causing organisms), helping the body to make vitamin K, maintaining the acid balance of the gut and keeping the immune system properly primed. Studies also suggest that upping your intake of natural probiotics – that is, from food, rather than supplements – might be a way of protecting yourself against colds and flu.

Always opt for products from natural sources uncontaminated by pesticides or toxins. I like fermented foods that are raw, organic

and unpasteurised, because the fermentation process concentrates everything contained in the food – pesticides included! If you're making your own fermented foods from a starter culture, look for one that includes *Lactobacillus plantarum*, one of the hardiest strains of good bacteria. Scientific studies suggest that this strain is particularly beneficial for intestinal health, has anti-viral properties and withstands the chemicals that usually kill probiotics, such as antibiotics, fluoride, chlorinated water and even stomach acid.

But for probiotics to do their good work, you need to eat prebiotic-rich foods as often as you consume probiotic-rich foods. Prebiotics are like motor oil for the body: high in fibre, which plays a key role in our gut and digestive systems, they keep everything lubricated and running well. One of the simplest ways to get more prebiotics in your diet is to regularly eat onions, garlic, leeks, shallots and chives – the medicinal properties of these members of the allium family have been known for centuries. Other prebiotic-rich foods include dandelion greens and Jerusalem artichokes.

These foods don't get fully digested by the acids and enzymes in our digestive tract, so they become 'fuel' for the beneficial bacteria, which then thrive and multiply. Essentially, what this leads to is a healthier digestive system and a greater diversity of bacteria living in our gut.

Just remember:
PREBIOTICS + PROBIOTICS = BETTER HEALTH

BONE BROTH: BREWING THE BENEFITS

Ever since our ancestors learned how to cook with fire about one million years ago, a pot of boiling broth over the flames has been a trait distinct to humans. There is archaeological evidence to suggest that people used reptile shells and the stomachs of animals they had killed as vessels in which to boil liquid, and that we knew how to boil water long before the invention of pottery (about 6000 BC). Not only does bone broth represent one of our most venerable culinary traditions, it's also nature's ultimate multivitamin and mineral supplement. Bone broth is full of minerals in a form that is much easier for us to digest than any plant source. These include phosphorus, magnesium, silicon, sulphur and other trace minerals, such as copper.

I generally make a big brew of bone broth in the slow cooker once a week and divide it up into portions (often freezing the leftovers, as it only lasts about three to four days in the fridge), so I can have a bit of broth each day. The difference between bone broth and stock is the lengthy simmering, with animal bones, herbs and vegetables being cooked together for at least 12 hours. This slow cooking breaks down

the collagen in the bones to gelatin, which acts to strengthen the gut in several ways. As well as containing the amino acid glycine, which enhances our stomach acid secretions and restores a healthy lining to the stomach, gelatin absorbs water, helping to keep the digestive tract healthy, as well as promoting good intestinal and bowel health.

BEVERAGES: BENEFITS AND PITFALLS

Drinking plenty of water is important for cellular regeneration and overall good health. While herbal teas can be very comforting and supportive for the body, especially when it comes to enhancing rest and relaxation, water remains my preferred drink.

Conversely, caffeinated beverages, such as coffee, tea and some soft drinks, may affect insulin levels, so it probably makes sense to minimise your caffeine intake.

Even more important, though, is to steer clear of sugar-free beverages that are being touted as a 'healthier' alternative manufactured by soft drink companies. The most recent findings suggest that drinking artificially sweetened soft drinks might dramatically increase the risk of type 2 diabetes. What's more, the mechanism involved is believed to be linked to changes in our gut bacteria caused by these beverages – another very good reason to give them a wide berth.

FASTING: A BEGINNER'S GUIDE

Fasting is the ultimate way to limit and help control the body's insulin production, and the latest scientific research suggests that fasting could play a part in the prevention of many conditions, especially obesity and type 2 diabetes. New research suggests that restricting the number of insulin-spiking carbohydrates and excess protein by intermittent fasting is one of the best ways we can live a healthy life. It's only in the last 50 years that fasting has stopped being used as a healing modality in the western world, but it's free and easy, and all you need is a little bit of information to get going.

What fasting does is stop the body from needing to produce insulin for the period of the fast. By fasting intermittently, we are able to normalise our blood-sugar levels and lose weight, because fasting teaches our body to produce only the insulin it needs to function (something our bodies do naturally, unless the process is disrupted by too many starchy and sugary foods). A low-carb lifestyle works in a similar way, offering an impressive 70 per cent of the insulin-lowering ability of fasting. Used in tandem, the two are very effective: a low-carb diet makes fasting easier

because you've already turned on your fat-burning switch, while fasting enables your body to get the maximum benefits from eating in this way. Several programs pairing fasting with a low-carb lifestyle have had success with helping people with metabolic diseases such as type 2 diabetes more effectively manage their condition.

An easy way to fast intermittently is to eat your evening meal before 6 pm and then delay your first meal of the next day until 10 am, so you fast for a period of 16 hours overnight – this can be done daily as there are no negative health consequences to eating only during eight hours of the day. Look at our meal plan (page 41) if you want to give it a go – and if you don't think you can skip breakfast entirely, then perhaps try one of our bone broths or soups instead.

Of course, it's best to work with your healthcare professional to find a way of fasting that's right for you, especially if you take regular medication. Note that fasting is *not* recommended for babies, children, teenagers, elderly people, pregnant women, type 1 diabetics or those with hypoglycaemia.

EAT WITH THE SEASONS

Whenever we eat, our metabolic rate increases, and this causes a slight rise in our body temperature. But according to the ancient Indian practice of Ayurveda, we can balance the chemical reactions caused by the digestive process simply by paying a little more attention to the types of foods we eat during each season.

Ayurvedic medicine was developed in India more than 3000 years ago, and is still practised today. As in many traditional healthcare systems, foods are classified as cooling or warming, and it's considered beneficial to eat food that has the right properties for each season. For example, on a hot summer's night, if we eat salad and lightly steamed veggies with lots of cooling in-season veggies, such as cucumbers, the high water content of these vegetables helps the body to stay cool and hydrated. By contrast, eating lots of curries and hearty stews in the winter, loaded with vegetables, herbs and medicinal spices such as turmeric, will help to reduce inflammation and support a stronger gut and thus a healthier immune system.

Remember the 12 new rules of nutrition

1 Go low carb, higher fat

2 Abandon sugar

3 Avoid processed and genetically modified foods

4 Embrace healthy fats, including eggs

5 Eat lots of greens and good veggies

6 Ditch dairy products

7 Evict grains and legumes

8 Learn to love fermented foods, and eat some fermented veggies at every meal

9 Drink plenty of good-quality water

10 Make friends with bone broth

11 Maintain a moderate intake of sustainable protein foods

12 Consider intermittent fasting

THE OTHER CORNERSTONES OF GOOD HEALTH

Along with learning to eat in a way that nourishes our bodies and minds, we also need to train ourselves to rest and sleep well, to move and exercise regularly, and to live mindfully. These are some of the healthiest habits you can adopt, and will make all the difference as you embark on a low-carb lifestyle.

RESTING

We all need a consistent six to eight hours sleep a night, but in today's 24/7 world our brains are finding it tougher than ever to switch off. Unfortunately, this means that insomnia, sleep deprivation and poor sleeping habits are becoming more prevalent. When we sleep we repair and detoxify, so if our sleep is often disrupted, this adversely affects our immune system and metabolism, and can ultimately lead to disease. Several studies have now proven a link between poor sleep and the development of obesity and type 2 diabetes. Sleep deprivation also causes insulin resistance. Losing sleep is a vicious and unhealthy cycle – but the good news is that making a few small changes can have a big impact on helping your body and brain to rest easy.

Stick to a sleep schedule

If you can, get to bed before 11 pm, as this is when our brains slow down enough to put us into a deep, restful sleep.

Sleep in a dark room

Sleeping in a totally dark room or with a sleep mask helps to regulate the production of melatonin, the hormone that helps us fall asleep. If you are a shift worker, it's even more important that your bedroom is completely dark, to give you the best chance of regulating your sleep cycles.

Make your bedroom an electronics-free zone

To create a calm environment for sleeping, it's a good idea to keep TVs and other electronic devices out of the bedroom altogether. You might also want to consider implementing a digital detox for at least two hours before bedtime. The screens of TVs, computers, smartphones and video games are made up of light-emitting diodes (LEDs) that produce lots of blue light, which has been shown to inhibit the production of melatonin. Blue light–blocking glasses are useful if you're watching television or looking at a screen at night; we use these at home ourselves.

Avoid caffeine and other stimulants

If you are having issues sleeping, it's a good idea to minimise your intake of caffeine and other stimulants, especially in the afternoon. It also helps to avoid alcohol, which contributes to poorer-quality sleep, with more frequent waking.

Get some daylight

Getting sunlight on your skin boosts vitamin D levels, and daylight helps to establish a normal circadian rhythm. Try to get outside for about 10–20 minutes in the morning or later in the afternoon, when the sun is less fierce; if you spend longer periods outdoors, make sure you cover up and use a natural non-toxic sunscreen.

Choose a comfy bed

We spend a third of our lives in bed, so it is just common sense to choose your mattress and pillows carefully, and to go with what gives you the greatest sense of calm.

Sleep in a cool room

Studies have shown that the best sleeping temperature is about 17–19ºC, which may be a little cool for some, but try not to sleep under so many covers or blankets that you are sweating in bed.

MOVING

There are so many beneficial ways you can move your body to take care of your health and wellbeing. Exercising every day is one of the ways I support good mental and physical health, and is honestly one of my favourite things to do ... next to cooking, of course. I'm not so much of a gym guy; instead, I like to get outdoors, because not only does a regular dip or paddle in the surf help to maintain my fitness levels but it also gets me into the ocean and in touch with nature, which is beneficial in so many ways.

Walk this way

If you need to develop your fitness, start with walking: you can walk outside on a nice day, or inside on a stormy one. For the first six weeks, aim to go walking between three and six days a week for 15–30 minutes a day. Begin on flat ground and build up to more hilly terrain. It's amazing what walking up a slight gradient can do for your core abdominal muscles too – worth keeping in mind if you want to cultivate toned abs!

Step it up: high-intensity cardio

After six weeks of walking, your fitness levels will be building, so it's a good time to add in 5–10 minutes of high-intensity cardio daily, if you want to. Very short bursts of high-intensity cardio get the heart pumping and blood flowing around the body. My favourite type of cardio is running around with the dog, skipping or jumping on the trampoline for 5–10 minutes. I also like to include a few exercise sessions at home each week for increased strength and fitness, such as squats, pull-ups, push-ups and core work. Just remember to warm up beforehand to reduce the risk of injury. Alternatively, yoga, swimming or surfing can quickly build up stamina and cardiovascular strength – and dancing and sex are wonderful and natural ways of raising your heartbeat in a holistic way.

Don't 'over-train'

If you have unrealistic expectations and try to push yourself too hard, the results can be very damaging. With high-intensity cardio, it's important not to over-train: too much high-intensity exercise can push our stress response too far, with detrimental effects on our health and wellbeing. Over-exertion can also cause our bodies to release too much of the stress hormone cortisol, contributing to sleep disturbances, depression and weight gain. Instead, remember that the aim is simply to move your body in a way that you love every day!

LIVING MINDFULLY

One of the healthiest habits you can adopt, alongside eating, sleeping and exercising regularly, is to live more mindfully. Mindfulness views the self as a harmonious whole, and teaches us that by 'observing' our behaviours we can choose to act, rather than react.

Breathing

Learning to breathe deeply is one of the most powerful ways we can take control of our own health. Not only does our breath contain vital oxygen, nitrogen and carbon dioxide to fuel our cells, but in eastern philosophies it also has a life force that energises our body, mind and soul. By concentrating on our breath, we effectively slow down the rate of our breathing and eventually we can more easily choose to stay in a calm, peaceful state.

Meditation

Recent scientific studies have confirmed that regular meditation can actually help to restore and even promote the growth of new neural pathways in the brain, and ongoing research suggests that meditation is one of the healthiest things we can do for body, mind and soul.

Set aside just 3 minutes a day at first. Choose a quiet corner and lay out a rug or mat. You can either sit cross-legged on a cushion or lie down with a cushion underneath your knees to support your back. If you need some help switching off from your surroundings, you might want to consider popping on some comfortable noise-cancelling headphones, and maybe even an eye mask. Now, begin to breathe deeply: inhale slowly through your nose, so that your diaphragm drops and your stomach expands as you fill your lungs; then exhale through your nose, pulling your belly button back in. As you breathe like this, centre and focus your mind on the breath and allow feelings of love and compassion to flow through you. Gradually build up to 15 minutes a day, and you'll be surprised at the transformation.

Mindfulness

This is as simple as being aware of our thoughts and feelings and accepting them, no matter what the situation. Mindfulness is about not judging ourselves, but instead paying attention to how our thought patterns influence our life. By letting go of what doesn't serve us, we are able to grow as individuals, reduce stress, enjoy more loving relationships and live more productive lives.

Living in a mindful way is proven to help increase our ability to feel compassionate towards ourselves and others, and to reduce the load on our brains that comes from being frazzled, stressed and full of guilt. It's all about cultivating an ongoing sense of calm. What could be more vital than that?

COOKING THE LOW-CARB, HEALTHY-FAT WAY

Now it's time to get into the kitchen and start cooking! To help you embrace a long-term, low-carb lifestyle, I've devised more than 130 easy new recipes. Everything from the ingredients in these dishes to the way they are cooked and served is about creating better health and wellbeing for you and your family for the rest of your lives.

My rule of thumb is to cook a small to moderate amount of well-sourced animal protein – such as chicken with the skin on, lamb chops or bacon, a delicious piece of fish with the skin on, or organic eggs – in good-quality fats or oils, then add some delicious colourful vegetables, either raw or cooked, with some fermented veg on the side.

It's also important to eat your meals in a quiet place, away from distractions, and to concentrate on really chewing your food. For example, when I'm filming, I'll often head outside at mealtimes, kick my shoes off and feel the earth beneath my feet while I eat my meal. Chewing your food well gets the digestive juices flowing and starts the digestion process.

A word on the recipes in the Treats section: they are exactly that ... TREATS! All sugar is sugar – whether it's honey, cane sugar or coconut sugar – and will raise your blood-sugar levels. You can opt for naturally occurring sweeteners, such as birch xylitol, green leaf stevia, monk fruit or liquid stevia. But while some of these won't raise blood-sugar levels, it's important to remember that adding any kind of sweet substance can make it far more difficult to kick a sugar addiction.

Treats are not a substitute for your daily fat, meat and vegetable intake, I am sorry to say. Your main source of nutrition should come from the aforementioned items, and you only need to look at the images in the Main Meals and Sides chapters to understand what your plates should look like. However, I also know that, from time to time, there are birthdays, anniversaries, work parties, date nights, school functions and fêtes where people like to enjoy a treat. I have endeavoured to include a selection of treats that are the least inflammatory for the body and offer some good fatty options with a lower carb content, to give the body the best chance of continuing good health. If you think eating one of these could kickstart your sugar addiction, perhaps abstain completely for as long as necessary. But if you are happy to indulge without falling off the wagon, then you may wish to try these for yourself and your family.

Once you get into the habit of cooking and eating this way at every meal, you will truly be eating like royalty, and food will never have tasted so good. So let's get cracking with some recipes, shall we?

TWO-WEEK LOW-CARB, HEALTHY-FAT MEAL PLAN

The following meal plan is simply a guide using recipes from this book, so feel free to swap out recipes and just eat meat and three veg for a meal. Meals can be as easy as gluten-free sausages with avocado, broccoli and onions or a simple omelette with vegetables, and you can always eat the same meal for the whole day if you like. I often do this; if I make a big soup, stew or curry, then I will eat it for my first meal as well as the next one later in the day. Just do whatever works best for you with the time and resources that you have. A good idea is to cook twice as much as you need for dinner, so you can take leftovers to work the next day for lunch.

Have a big glass of water with lemon or vinegar in the morning, and remember to stay hydrated throughout the day. I also recommend incorporating a cup of bone broth into your daily diet, and adding some fermented veggies to each meal (starting off with just ½ teaspoon if you have never had them before and building up to about 1–2 tablespoons per meal).

Avoid treats for as long as possible, until blood-sugar levels are normal and intermittent fasting is comfortable – at least four to six weeks to give the body a good break.

MEAL-PLAN TIPS:

1 Pick a side to go with any of the meals (see pages 191–231).

2 Try to stick to a simple broth or soup in the morning, but it's best to get into the swing of intermittent fasting – so eating between 10 am and 6 pm or any other eight-hour window for your two meals a day.

3 If you need a snack, choose one from the Snacks (page 47) or Sides (page 191) chapters.

PLAN | week | ONE

	BREAKFAST	FIRST MEAL	SECOND MEAL
MONDAY	Fast or any bone broth, soup or smoothie	BLAT wrap (page 173)	Chicken marylands with salmoriglio (page 159)
TUESDAY	Fast or any bone broth, soup or smoothie	Avocado bun burger (page 160)	Pan-fried blue mackerel with pickled zucchini and almond aioli (page 133)
WEDNESDAY	Fast or any bone broth, soup or smoothie	Mushroom omelette with silverbeet (page 116)	Sirloin steak with furikake seasoning, bonito aioli and greens (page 188)
THURSDAY	Fast or any bone broth, soup or smoothie	Pork san choy bau with fried egg (page 162)	Roasted spiced salmon with grilled cos and green goddess dressing (page 145)
FRIDAY	Fast or any bone broth, soup or smoothie	Cauliflower and bacon toast with avocado and fried egg (page 118)	Roast pork belly salad with sesame dressing (page 170)
SATURDAY	Fast or any bone broth, soup or smoothie	Tuna poke with fried egg and coconut tortilla (page 139)	Curry beef pies (page 187)
SUNDAY	Fast or any bone broth, soup or smoothie	Prawn cocktail avo bowls (page 126)	Blood sausage with fried egg and chimichurri (page 179)

PLAN week TWO

	BREAKFAST	FIRST MEAL	SECOND MEAL
MONDAY	Fast or any bone broth, soup or smoothie	Pickled beetroot eggs with smoked salmon and avocado salad (page 140)	Chicken wings with tomato, basil and greens (page 150)
TUESDAY	Fast or any bone broth, soup or smoothie	Green omelette with oven-baked tomato, mushrooms and bacon (page 115)	Zucchini noodles with tuna, chilli, rocket and capers (page 134)
WEDNESDAY	Fast or any bone broth, soup or smoothie	Eggs florentine with baked mushrooms (page 125)	Pork sausages with kraut and mustard (page 167)
THURSDAY	Fast or any bone broth, soup or smoothie	Chorizo mince with fried eggs and leafy greens (page 168)	Togarashi snapper with sautéed greens and curry mayonnaise (page 146)
FRIDAY	Fast or any bone broth, soup or smoothie	Savoury granola breakfast bowl (page 110)	Spiced pork chops with apple and rhubarb salsa (page 176)
SATURDAY	Fast or any bone broth, soup or smoothie	Spiced egg curry (page 121)	Zucchetti aglio e olio with prawns (page 128)
SUNDAY	Fast or any bone broth, soup or smoothie	Pork belly terrine (page 164)	Chicken basque with olives and artichokes (page 156)

PART two

LOW-CARB, HEALTHY-FAT RECIPES

SNACKS
SOUPS
MAIN MEALS
SIDES
TREATS
DRINKS
FATS
BASICS

1

SNACKS

AVOCADO HUMMUS

SERVES 4

2 avocados, sliced

3 tablespoons extra-virgin olive oil,
   plus extra to serve

2 tablespoons hulled tahini

3 tablespoons lemon juice

2 garlic cloves, chopped

½ teaspoon ground cumin

pinch of cayenne pepper (optional)

sea salt and freshly ground
   black pepper

TO SERVE

Coconut Flour Pita Bread
   (page 285)

lemon wedges

When avocados are abundant and cheap, it's a good idea to stock up the freezer with some of their fatty goodness. Make this avocado hummus in bulk and freeze in small portions so you can grab some in the morning and pop it in the fridge, then when you get home, it will have thawed and you'll have some lovely good-quality fat for your family to snack on. Here, I have teamed the hummus with paleo pita bread, but you could serve it with carrot, celery, cucumber, olives, fennel, radishes, lettuce and seed crackers, or on the side of a grilled piece of fish or meat.

Place the avocado, olive oil, tahini, lemon juice, garlic, cumin and cayenne pepper (if using) in the bowl of a food processor and blend until smooth and creamy. Season with salt and pepper. If the hummus is too thick, mix in a little cold water.

Spoon the hummus into a serving dish, drizzle over a little extra olive oil, sprinkle on a pinch of salt and pepper and serve with the pita bread and lemon wedges.

WARM MARINATED OLIVES WITH ROSEMARY, GARLIC AND PINE NUTS

SERVES 4

1 teaspoon fennel seeds
1 teaspoon coriander seeds
250 g mixed olives
½ orange, peeled, zest cut into
    1 cm strips (optional)
100 ml extra-virgin olive oil
1 ½ tablespoons sherry vinegar
1 garlic clove, finely chopped
1 long red chilli, sliced
1–2 rosemary sprigs, broken into
    smaller lengths
2 tablespoons pine nuts, toasted
sea salt and freshly ground
    black pepper

One of my all-time favourite foods on the planet is the humble olive. I am so stoked that my eldest daughter, Chilli, has discovered them and appreciates them … so much so that she can eat a whole jar in one sitting! You don't have to do much to olives to make them shine, but if you wish to add a little extra sparkle, try this simple recipe to bring a depth of flavour that can become very addictive. Olives make for a wonderful addition to school lunch boxes. Remember: olives are a fruit, so there is nothing the teachers can get upset about.

Place the fennel and coriander seeds in a frying pan and toast over medium heat, shaking the pan often to evenly distribute the seeds, for 30 seconds–1 minute until fragrant. Transfer to a mortar and pound with the pestle until coarsely crushed.

Combine the olives, orange zest (if using), olive oil, vinegar, garlic, chilli and rosemary in a bowl. Add the crushed toasted seeds and mix well. Marinate for at least 1 hour or, for best results, overnight in the fridge.

Place the olive mixture and pine nuts in a saucepan and gently cook over low heat for 3–5 minutes to warm the olives. (Don't allow the oil to go over 100°C. You don't want it to burn.) Season to taste with salt and pepper and serve warm, with a small bowl for the olive pits.

PORK CRACKLING (CHICHARRONES)

SERVES 4

1 kg pork back fat, skin on, cut in half
coconut oil or good-quality animal
  fat*, melted, for deep-frying
sea salt
apple cider vinegar, for dipping

* See Glossary

Are you serious, Evans? You mean to say we can eat pork crackling and it is actually good for us? Well, yes, I consider it to be part of a healthy low-carb diet – and if you don't want to eat yours, then may I have it? I don't think anyone can resist well-cooked pork crackling when it is placed in front of them. My children beg for more whenever we serve up delicious roast pork, and there is never enough to go around. These days I buy more skin, so we have extra on hand for school lunch boxes or after-school snacks.

Preheat the oven to 120°C. Place a wire rack on a baking tray.

Half-fill a large saucepan with water, add the pork, bring to the boil and simmer for 15 minutes, to soften. (This helps loosen the fat when cutting.) Drain and allow to cool.

When cool enough to handle, using a sharp knife, cut the pork into long strips, about 5 cm wide. At one end of each pork strip, carefully insert the knife between the fat and skin and slice through to remove the layer of fat. If you still have a thin layer of fat left on the pork skin, again run your knife between the layer of fat and skin until the fat is removed. It's okay if there's still a thin layer of fat remaining. Reserve the fat trimmings to make lard (page 276).

Cut the pork skin into 4 cm squares and place, fat-side down (the side that the fat has been removed from), on the wire rack. Bake for 4–4 ½ hours until the skin has completely dried out and is hard. Scrape off the remaining fat after drying out if needed.

Pour the oil or fat into a large saucepan to a depth of 7.5 cm. Place over medium heat and heat to 180°C. To test if the oil is hot enough, place a small piece of skin in the pan. If the oil sizzles and the skin puffs up, it has reached its ideal temperature. Add the pork skin, in batches, and cook submerged in the oil for 3–5 minutes until puffed and golden. Carefully remove the pork skin from the pan using metal tongs or a slotted spoon and drain on paper towel. Sprinkle immediately with salt. Serve with some vinegar on the side for dipping.

BROCCOMOLE FAT BOMBS

MAKES 6

4 rindless bacon rashers
60 ml (¼ cup) coconut oil, melted
1 x Broccomole (page 203)

Fat and greens are the ticket to health with a low-carb approach, and you are going to love these morsels as a satisfying and delicious snack or even as a side to a piece of grilled fish, chicken or steak. I recommend making a double batch, so you have some on hand for a quick breakfast or for when the kids get home from school. You can also add hard-boiled eggs to the mix, too!

Preheat the oven to 180°C. Grease and line a large baking tray with baking paper.

Arrange the bacon on the prepared tray in a single layer, making sure that the strips are not touching. Bake, turning the tray once for even cooking, for 15–20 minutes until the bacon is golden and crisp. Keep a close eye on the bacon to prevent it from burning. Set aside to cool and reserve the bacon fat for the Broccomole.

Mix the coconut oil and reserved bacon fat through the Broccomole, cover with plastic wrap and place in the fridge for 20–30 minutes to firm up.

Meanwhile, chop the bacon into small pieces ready for crumbing.

Remove the Broccomole from the fridge and roll the mixture into six golf ball–sized balls. Roll each ball in the bacon bits to coat, then place back on a tray and refrigerate for 20–30 minutes until slightly firm.

Enjoy the fat bombs on their own or serve with a side of veggie sticks.

CHICKEN LIVER PÂTÉ

SERVES 4–6

2 tablespoons duck fat, tallow
   or coconut oil, melted
1 onion, chopped
4 garlic cloves, chopped
1 ½ teaspoons thyme leaves
2 bay leaves
4 sage leaves, chopped
125 ml (½ cup) red wine
   (such as shiraz)
125 ml (½ cup) bone marrow
   (ask the butcher to cut the
   marrow bone lengthways so the
   marrow is easier to scoop out)
   (or use duck fat, tallow or lard)
500 g chicken livers, trimmed
1 tablespoon Dijon mustard
50 ml Chicken Bone Broth
   (page 284)
sea salt and freshly ground
   black pepper

JELLY

4 thyme sprigs, leaves picked
250 ml (1 cup) Chicken Bone Broth
   (page 284)
½ tablespoon powdered gelatine

TO SERVE

seed and nut loaf or paleo bread,
   toasted, or seeded crackers
Sauerkraut (page 295)

We need to eat more offal, and pâté is the easiest and most subtle way for you to add it – in the form of liver – to your diet. In our house, we absolutely love liver and eat it at least three times a week. We make a big batch of pâté or terrine, then freeze it in small jars or portions so we can enjoy it as part of a meal, as a snack or as an amazing lunchtime treat. We like to serve ours with raw veg – like carrots, cucumber, celery, fennel and salad leaves – and paleo bread or seeded nut crackers with gherkins and fermented veg on the side. You can also use it in lettuce wraps (see banh mi on page 148) or try adding a spoonful to your chicken soup or bolognese sauce just before serving.

Place 1 tablespoon of the fat or oil, the onion, garlic and thyme in a saucepan over medium–low heat and cook, stirring occasionally, for 10–15 minutes until the onion has softened and slightly caramelised. Add the bay leaves and sage, pour in the wine and simmer until reduced to a glaze. Set aside to cool. Remove the bay leaves.

Scoop the marrow flesh from the bone and place it in a saucepan. Cook over medium–low heat for 15–20 minutes until the marrow turns to liquid, then allow to cool to lukewarm.

Heat the remaining fat or oil in a large frying pan over medium–high heat, add the livers in batches and cook for 30 seconds on each side until they are browned but still pink in the middle. Remove from the pan and set aside to cool.

Place the cooked livers, onion and wine reduction, mustard, marrow and broth in a blender and blend until smooth. Add salt to taste and blend a few times to mix through.

Pass the pâté through a fine sieve and add pepper to taste.

Spoon the pâté into jars or bowls, leaving 1.5 cm space at the top. Cover and place in the fridge for 4–6 hours to set.

For the jelly, combine the thyme and broth in a saucepan, bring to the boil and simmer until reduced by half. Meanwhile, sprinkle the gelatine over 3 tablespoons of water and set aside for 2 minutes. Add to the hot broth and stir until dissolved. Allow to cool completely before pouring over the pâté portions. Chill for 1 hour before serving.

Serve the pâté with toasted seed and nut loaf, paleo bread or seeded crackers of your choice and sauerkraut.

GRILLED CHORIZO WITH MOJO VERDE

SERVES 4

4 chorizo sausages
coconut oil or good-quality animal
    fat*, melted, for brushing

MOJO VERDE

4 garlic cloves, roughly chopped
80 g (2 firmly packed cups)
    coriander leaves
½ teaspoon ground cumin
1 long red chilli, deseeded
    and chopped
¼ teaspoon sea salt, plus extra
    if needed
125 ml (½ cup) extra-virgin olive oil
2 tablespoons apple cider vinegar
    or sherry vinegar

* See Glossary

Snags have been used as snacks ever since we learned how to make them. I love fresh and cured sausages, and you can use either for this recipe. If you use fresh chorizo, you need to cook it. I like to cook it whole, then slice it (some people prefer to slice it first, then cook the slices until crispy), as I've done here. If you are using cured chorizo, you can slice and serve it at room temperature, or you can fry it up a little. Make sure when you purchase or make your chorizo that you use only free-range pork.

Mojo verde is a Spanish green sauce you will fall in love with. It is so good on egg or vegetable dishes or just about any grilled meat or seafood – the fattier the meat or fish the better.

If you want to turn this into a bigger meal, the combination of chorizo with seafood or chicken works a treat, so play around with some ideas.

To make the mojo verde, place the garlic, coriander, cumin, chilli and salt in the bowl of a food processor and process, occasionally scraping down the side of the bowl, until the coriander is finely chopped. With the motor running, drizzle in the olive oil and vinegar and process until well blended. Season with extra salt if needed. Transfer to a bowl and set aside.

Preheat the oven to 220°C.

Heat a chargrill pan over high heat or a barbecue grill to hot, brush the chorizo with a little oil or fat and grill the sausages, turning regularly, for 2–3 minutes until charred. Transfer to a baking tray and bake in the oven, turning occasionally, for 5–8 minutes until deep golden brown and cooked through.

Slice the chorizo into 1 cm thick pieces and place on plates. Spoon over the mojo verde and serve.

AVOCADO DEVILLED EGGS

MAKES 12

6 eggs

1 avocado, chopped

2 tablespoons Mayonnaise
   (page 292)

1 ½ teaspoons lemon juice

1 tablespoon finely chopped
   flat-leaf parsley leaves,
   plus extra, roughly chopped,
   to serve

sea salt and freshly ground
   black pepper

1–2 tablespoons salmon roe

I know you and your family will love this recipe as much as we do. I mean, who wouldn't? Look at all the natural goodness here and tell me that doesn't excite you on so many levels. These devilled eggs are incredibly easy to make for a crowd, brimming with good fats and quality proteins, and extremely low carb, plus they will keep you feeling full for ages. I could go on and on … but you get the picture. Oh, and I almost forgot to mention that they are absolutely delicious.

Fill a saucepan with water and bring to the boil. Reduce the heat to medium so that the water is rapidly simmering, then add the eggs and cook for 8 minutes. Drain and, when cool enough to handle, peel the eggs under cold running water. Allow the eggs to cool completely.

Slice the eggs in half lengthways. Carefully remove the yolks from the whites and place the yolks in a bowl. Mash the yolks with a fork, add the avocado, mayonnaise, lemon juice and finely chopped parsley and whip with a spatula or wooden spoon until smooth and creamy. If you like, you can place the mixture in a food processor and blend until smooth. Season with a little salt and pepper, if needed.

Place the egg-white halves, cavity-side up, on a platter and evenly spoon the avocado mixture into the cavities. Top each filled egg with ½ teaspoon of salmon roe, scatter over the extra parsley leaves and serve.

HOMEMADE BACON

MAKES 1 KG

1 kg pork belly

3 tablespoons sea salt

2 tablespoons liquid smoke (optional)

1 tablespoon freshly ground black pepper

2 teaspoons finely chopped rosemary leaves

1 teaspoon finely chopped thyme leaves

1 teaspoon fennel seeds

2 garlic cloves, chopped

2 tablespoons honey (optional)

A lot of people find it difficult to source good-quality free-range bacon. Luckily for us, finding good-quality free-range pork belly is often easier. And once you have the pork belly, it is quite simple to turn it into bacon. Now, there is a little sweetener used in this recipe but, at the end of the day, you are eating just a slice or two of bacon, so it is quite negligible over a whole day of food intake. You can cut down the sweetness if you choose.

1 Rinse the pork belly in cold water and pat dry with paper towel. Place the pork in a large dish and set aside. To make the marinade, place the salt, liquid smoke (if using), pepper, rosemary, thyme, fennel seeds and garlic in a mortar and pound with a pestle to finely crush. Stir through the honey (if using) to combine.

2 Rub the marinade over the pork belly until completely coated. Cover and refrigerate for 1 week, flipping the pork every day.

3 Remove the pork from the dish, scrape off the marinade and rinse thoroughly in cold water.

4 Pat the pork dry with a clean cloth.

5 Preheat the oven to 90°C. Place a lightly greased wire rack on a baking tray. Place the cured pork belly, skin-side down, on the wire rack and roast for 2–2 1/4 hours, or until the internal temperature of the pork reaches 65°C. Remove from the oven and cool slightly. When cool enough to handle, transfer the pork to a chopping board and slice off the skin. Place the skin in an airtight container in the fridge and reserve for making crackling. Set the bacon aside at room temperature and allow to cool completely, then place in a container, cover and refrigerate for a few hours. Slice to your preferred thickness.

6 Place the bacon slices in a frying pan over medium heat and cook for a few minutes on each side until golden brown and crispy. Enjoy with eggs and your favourite sides, or add to any dishes you like. Store the remaining bacon in an airtight container in the fridge for up to 2 weeks or freeze for up to 3 months.

STEP 1

STEP 2

STEP 3

STEP 4

STEP 5

STEP 6

BROCCOLI AND BACON SKEWERS

SERVES 4–6

5 rindless streaky bacon rashers,
   cut in half crossways,
   then halved lengthways
1 head of broccoli (about 300 g),
   cut into 20 florets
1 tablespoon coconut oil or
   good-quality animal fat*, melted
sea salt and freshly ground
   black pepper
juice of ½ lemon
100 g Aioli (page 280)
2 pinches of smoked paprika

* See Glossary

Everyone knows that everything tastes better when bacon is added. So, what better way to make the kids enjoy their greens than by wrapping them in crispy bacon? This concept is nothing new: I remember as an apprentice chef close to 30 years ago wrapping prosciutto around asparagus. At the time this was called fancy food or nouvelle cuisine! You can try this simple and tasty recipe with different types of veg. Cauliflower, mushrooms, green beans, asparagus, pumpkin and Jerusalem artichokes all work well, but my all-time favourite has to be broccoli. You will need to soak 20 bamboo skewers in water for 10–20 minutes for this recipe.

Preheat the oven to 200°C. Line a baking tray with baking paper.

Wrap a bacon strip around each broccoli floret, then carefully insert a skewer through the bacon and broccoli to hold them in place.

Place the bacon and broccoli skewers on the prepared tray in a single layer, approximately 1 cm apart, to help them cook evenly. Drizzle with the oil or fat and sprinkle on some salt and pepper. Bake for 20 minutes until the broccoli is cooked through and the bacon is golden and crispy.

Transfer the bacon and broccoli skewers to a platter and squeeze over some lemon juice. Spoon the aioli into a small serving bowl, sprinkle on the smoked paprika and serve with the skewers.

NOTE
Biltong is traditionally hung and air-dried for a few days in a humidity- and temperature-controlled room, but the oven method used here is more practical for making this at home.

BILTONG

SERVES 10–15

2 tablespoons coriander seeds
1 tablespoon sea salt
1 tablespoon coconut sugar
1½ teaspoons freshly ground
  black pepper
1 teaspoon bicarbonate of soda
2 teaspoons smoked paprika
1 teaspoon chilli flakes (optional)
700 g beef sirloin
80 ml (⅓ cup) apple cider vinegar
coconut oil, for greasing

It is amazing how old-school foods are enjoying a resurgence around the world. Biltong, with its amazing texture and flavour, is one of my favourites. A South African national dish, it is basically a chewy and addictive generously spiced piece of dried beef. I often travel with biltong when I am away from home and do not know if I will have access to good-quality fresh meat. I find this to be a wonderful substitute and never tire of it. If you are keen, you can buy specialised biltong-drying machines, or you can use a food dehydrator or simply your oven on very low.

Heat a frying pan over medium heat, add the coriander seeds and toast, tossing occasionally, for 1–2 minutes until fragrant and lightly golden. Allow to cool, then crush the toasted coriander seeds using a mortar and pestle. Mix with the salt, coconut sugar, pepper, bicarb soda, paprika and chilli flakes (if using). Set aside.

Trim and remove any fat, sinew and gristle from the beef. (This helps the drying process and ensures the final product lasts longer without being extremely tough to eat. Leaving too much fat on the meat can cause spoilage during the drying process, so it's important to remove all visible fat.) Cut or bash the beef into 2.5 cm thick slices roughly 20 cm long, depending on the length of your piece of sirloin.

Pour half the vinegar into a large, deep tray or dish and evenly sprinkle over 2 tablespoons of the coriander seasoning. Add the slices of meat in a single layer, then drizzle the remaining vinegar over the meat and sprinkle over some more seasoning. Flip the meat over, so the vinegar evenly coats it, and continue seasoning and flipping the meat until all the seasoning is used and the meat is well coated. Cover the tray with plastic wrap and refrigerate for 24 hours, flipping the meat every few hours to allow it to marinate evenly.

Preheat the oven to 70°C. Lightly grease a wire rack with coconut oil and place it on a baking tray.

Remove the beef from the marinade and place on the rack. Transfer to the oven and bake for 10–12 hours until the meat is completely dried out.

Cut the biltong into pieces to serve. Store in an airtight container in the fridge for up to 1 month or freeze, ideally in a vacuum-sealed bag, for 6 months.

ROASTED BONE MARROW WITH PARSLEY AND PICKLED SHALLOT SALAD

SERVES 4

1 kg centre-cut beef marrow bones, cut into 3 cm pieces, tendons trimmed (ask your butcher to do this)

sea salt

8 thin slices of seed and nut loaf, toasted, to serve

PARSLEY AND PICKLED SHALLOT SALAD

2 French shallots, sliced

3 tablespoons apple cider vinegar

2 handfuls of flat-leaf parsley leaves

1 tablespoon salted baby capers, rinsed and patted dry

2 spring onions, green part only, thinly sliced

1 ½ teaspoons extra-virgin olive oil

freshly ground black pepper

Bone marrow is delicious! I like to scrape it out of the bone and add its fatty richness to my soups and sauces – like bolognese or the filling for a cottage or shepherd's pie – for extra depth of flavour (my kids don't even know they are eating it). And, of course, when we have guests over we love to serve it like this, alongside some other goodies such as fermented veg and a nice salad. Always make sure you ask your butcher for grass-fed and grass-finished bone marrow.

To make the pickled shallot, place the shallot and vinegar in a small saucepan and bring to the boil over medium–high heat. Remove from the heat and set aside to pickle for at least 30 minutes. For best results, cover and leave overnight in the fridge. Drain and set aside, reserving both the vinegar and the shallots for the parsley salad.

Preheat the oven to 200°C.

Place the marrow bones on a baking tray and season with salt. Roast for 15 minutes until golden brown and cooked through.

To make the salad, combine the parsley, capers, spring onion, olive oil and pickled shallots in a bowl, add 1 teaspoon of the reserved vinegar from the pickled shallot, toss well and season with salt and pepper.

Place the roasted bone marrow on serving plates, add a handful of the parsley salad and serve with the toasted seed and nut loaf.

BACON-WRAPPED AVOCADO FRIES WITH NORI MAYONNAISE

SERVES 2

1 large avocado, halved

10 thin rindless streaky
    bacon rashers

1 teaspoon finely chopped nori*
    (approximately ½ sheet)

80 g Mayonnaise (page 292)

sea salt and freshly ground
    black pepper

1 lemon wedge

2 pinches of shichimi togarashi*
    (optional)

* See Glossary

I am sure this recipe will become a new favourite in your household once you give it a try. This is so delicious and wonderful to create when avocados are plentiful. Always use free-range bacon with no nasties added, or you can try the simple bacon recipe we have shared on page 62. You can simplify this by making bacon chips and serving them with guacamole. Perfect for breakfast in summer or as a finger-food snack after school.

Slice the avocado lengthways into ten 1 cm thick pieces and set aside.

Preheat the oven to 200°C. Line a baking tray with baking paper.

Arrange the bacon pieces in a single layer on the prepared tray. Transfer to the oven for 1 minute to soften. When cool enough to handle, carefully wrap one strip of bacon around one piece of avocado, starting at the bottom of the avocado piece and wrapping all the way to the top. Tuck the end of the bacon under the avocado so that it's well secured. Continue with the remaining pieces of bacon and avocado.

Place the bacon-wrapped avocado pieces on the baking tray and bake for 15–20 minutes until the bacon is lightly golden and crispy.

Meanwhile, mix the nori and mayonnaise in a bowl and season with a touch of salt and pepper.

Arrange the avocado fries on a platter, squeeze over some lemon juice, then sprinkle on some shichimi togarashi (if using). Serve the nori mayonnaise on the side for dipping.

MINCE JERKY

MAKES 20–30 PIECES

2 tablespoons tamari or
    coconut aminos*
1 teaspoon sea salt, plus extra
    if needed
1 teaspoon freshly ground
    black pepper
1 teaspoon garlic powder
1 teaspoon smoked paprika
    (or your favourite spice, such as
    chilli powder or ground cumin)
800 g beef, lamb, kangaroo,
    emu or venison mince

* See Glossary

Beef jerky is wonderful to make and delicious to eat, and comes in handy for school or work lunches and long road or plane trips. This recipe uses minced meat instead of the usual sirloin or other expensive cuts of beef. Minced meat already has the fat added, giving the jerky a much better flavour. Give this a whirl and play around with different spices.

Preheat the oven to 70°C. Line two baking trays with baking paper.

Mix the tamari or coconut aminos, salt, pepper, garlic powder and smoked paprika with the mince to combine.

Divide the mince mixture between the prepared trays. Press down with your hands and flatten the mince on each tray into a large patty, then cover with a sheet of baking paper. Using a rolling pin, roll out the mince between the sheets of baking paper to form a thin even layer, about 2 mm thick. Peel away the top sheet of baking paper and discard.

Transfer the mince to the oven for 8–10 hours, flipping the meat over halfway, until completely dried out and hard.

Break the mince jerky into small pieces or cut into bite-sized squares. Add a little salt, if desired. Store in an airtight container in the fridge for up to 3 weeks.

PEMMICAN (AKA 'THE KETO BOMB')

MAKES 20–30 PIECES

1 ½ tablespoons ground turmeric
1 teaspoon finely grated ginger
1 teaspoon garlic powder
1 teaspoon onion powder
3 teaspoons mixed dried herbs
  (or any fresh or dried herbs
  of your choice)
1 kg beef mince
500 g tallow (see Note)
sea salt and freshly ground
  black pepper

Pemmican, a native staple that has helped sustain the indigenous peoples of North America, is basically a mixture of animal protein and fat that, if properly made, can last for up to ten years. It really should become the new go-to snack to replace those sugar-laden protein bars that masquerade as health food. Give this recipe a try – it's a terrific and filling treat to have at work or school, when travelling or just at home.

Preheat the oven 70°C. Line a baking tray with baking paper. Line a 20 cm × 30 cm Swiss roll tin with baking paper.

Combine the turmeric, ginger, garlic powder, onion powder, herbs and beef in a bowl and mix well.

Place the beef mixture on the prepared tray, press the mince down, then cover with a sheet of baking paper. Using a rolling pin, roll out the meat to form a thin even layer, about 1 cm thick. (If the meat is too thick, you may need to transfer some of the mixture to a second tray and repeat this process.) Peel off the top sheet of paper and transfer the tray to the oven for 10–12 hours, flipping the meat over after 5–6 hours, until the mince is completely dried out and hard.

Place the tallow in a saucepan and melt over low heat. Allow to cool to lukewarm.

Place the dried meat in the bowl of a food processor and process for 1–2 minutes until a fine crumb forms. Pour in the melted tallow and continue to process until combined. Season with salt and pepper. Pour into the prepared tin and spread the mixture out evenly with a palette knife. Transfer to the fridge to set for at least 1–1 ½ hours. Cut into bite-sized squares or finger-sized bars and serve. Keep stored in the fridge for up to 2 weeks.

NOTE
Tallow (rendered beef fat) can be purchased from your butcher. You may need to order it in advance. Go for tallow made from organic, grass-fed beef if you can. You can also try making your own (see recipe page 276).

TIP
You can also add some chopped offal, such as heart, liver or kidneys, with your mince. I like to use 50 per cent beef mince/50 per cent offal.

PRAWN AND SALMON TARTARE WITH AVOCADO CREAM AND NORI CRISPS

SERVES 4

150 g (1 ½ cups) tapioca flour*,
   plus extra for dusting
200 ml ice-cold sparkling
   mineral water
3 nori sheets*
melted coconut oil, for frying
sea salt
150 g cooked or raw peeled prawns
200 g sashimi-grade salmon
3 tablespoons Mayonnaise
   (page 292)
½ teaspoon finely grated ginger
2 teaspoons yuzu juice* or
   lemon juice
1 Lebanese cucumber, deseeded
   and cut into small dice

AVOCADO CREAM

1 avocado, roughly chopped
½ teaspoon wasabi (optional)
1 teaspoon yuzu juice* or
   lemon juice
freshly ground black pepper

TO SERVE

2 tablespoons salmon roe
baby shiso leaves or
   coriander leaves
toasted black and white
   sesame seeds
1 tablespoon tamari or
   coconut aminos*
1 tablespoon extra-virgin olive oil

* See Glossary

This could also be a main meal, as it is quite filling when combined with a lovely salad or some vegetables. Salmon tartare is a classic French dish that can easily be changed by adding different spices and herbs to give it a completely new feel. Here, in my Japanese version, I have added crispy nori for a fun textural component. But you don't need to crisp the nori; instead you might like to tear off a piece about the size of your palm, place some tartare in the middle, roll it up and pop it in your mouth like a classic hand roll.

Place the tapioca flour in a bowl and slowly whisk in the mineral water. Continue whisking until the batter has the consistency of pouring cream.

Lightly dust the nori with the extra tapioca flour and set aside.

Add the coconut oil to a depth of 10 cm to a wok or large saucepan and heat to 160°C. (To test if the oil is the right temperature, dip a small piece of nori in the batter, then add to the oil; if it bubbles around the edges, the oil is ready.) Working in batches, dip the nori pieces, one at a time, in the batter to coat completely, then carefully slide into the hot oil. (The nori will become very soft very quickly once it is coated with batter, so it's best to fry immediately.) Fry the nori on both sides until pale golden – 40–60 seconds on each side. Drain on paper towel and sprinkle with salt. If the nori is soft when cool, cook for a little longer in the hot oil. Break into pieces once cooled.

To make the avocado cream, place the avocado, wasabi (if using) and yuzu or lemon juice in a bowl. Mash and mix well with a fork until creamy. Season with salt and pepper.

To make the tartare, finely dice the prawns and salmon and place in a chilled bowl. Mix in the mayonnaise, ginger, yuzu or lemon juice and cucumber and season with salt and pepper.

Place a 7 cm ring mould on each serving plate, spoon in the tartare and press down to shape into a neat round. Remove the ring mould and spread some avocado cream on top of each tartare. Dot with the salmon roe, sprinkle on the shiso or coriander leaves and sesame seeds, drizzle on the tamari or coconut aminos and olive oil and serve with the nori crisps on the side.

SPICY TUNA ON CRISPY BACON CHIPS

MAKES ABOUT 30

230 g (about 8 slices) rindless
    streaky bacon
50 g Mayonnaise (page 292)
micro coriander leaves, to serve

SPICY TUNA

3 tablespoons Sriracha Chilli Sauce
    (page 296)
1 teaspoon finely grated ginger
1 tablespoon snipped chives
1 ½ tablespoons lemon juice
3 tablespoons extra-virgin
    olive oil
½ avocado, cut into small dice
100 g sashimi-grade tuna,
    cut into 5 mm dice
100 g canned tuna, in brine, drained
sea salt and freshly ground
    black pepper

Crispy bacon chips topped with a little seafood mix is just the ticket when you want to prepare a tasty snack for any occasion. This super-easy recipe is so delicious and so very, very satisfying. You can make it with either raw or cooked tuna – or both, as I've done here. Or try it with another seafood altogether.

Preheat the oven to 200°C. Grease a large baking tray and line with baking paper.

Place the bacon in a single layer on the prepared tray, making sure that the strips are not touching. Bake, turning the tray once for an even cook, for 20–25 minutes until the bacon is golden and crisp. Keep a close eye on the bacon to prevent it from burning. Drain the bacon oil from the tray and reserve for cooking. Drain the bacon on paper towel. Allow to cool completely, then cut into bite-sized pieces. Set aside.

To make the spicy tuna, place the sriracha, ginger, chives, lemon juice and olive oil in a bowl and mix well. Divide the sriracha mixture between two bowls, then divide the avocado between each bowl. Add the raw tuna to one bowl and gently toss to combine. Add the canned tuna to the other bowl and mix well. Season with salt and pepper.

Place the bacon chips on a platter and top each with a teaspoon of mayonnaise. Add a spoonful of raw spicy tuna to half the bacon chips and a spoonful of canned spicy tuna to the other half, or you can mix both together. Scatter on the micro coriander and serve.

KALE CHIPS

SERVES 2

1 bunch of curly kale (about 350 g)
1 tablespoon melted coconut oil
½ teaspoon of your favourite spice
(such as curry powder, ras el
hanout, smoked paprika,
ground cumin or ground
turmeric) (optional)
sea salt

Kale chips are a wonderful snack to make when kale is abundant or if you have some leftover in the fridge. I always recommend you use organic kale, rather than kale that has been sprayed with nasties. Have a play around with different spices and seasonings to mix things up from time to time. These never last long in our house and I am sure the same will happen for you.

Preheat the oven to 120°C. Line a baking tray with baking paper.

Wash the kale thoroughly with cold water and pat dry. Remove and discard the tough central stems, then cut the leaves into smaller pieces.

In a large bowl, toss the kale with some coconut oil, spice (if using) and salt – go easy on the salt as a little goes a long way. Spread the kale on the baking tray in a single layer; do not overcrowd. Use more than one baking tray, if required. Roast the kale for 35–40 minutes until crispy. Serve immediately or store in an airtight container in the pantry for up to 2 weeks.

BONE BROTH JELLIES

MAKES 14

125 ml (½ cup) filtered water
3 tablespoons powdered gelatine
300 ml Chicken, Beef or Fish Bone
    Broth (pages 284, 282 and 287)
pinch of sea salt

I know a lot of people don't feel like consuming broth when it is 30°C plus outside, so why not try making these little jellies as a snack instead? Now, they might seem a little strange at first ... but you will grow to enjoy cold broth or jellies once you become accustomed to them. If you are still not sold, then you can make these in muffin shapes or as a loaf and add some cooked chicken, boiled eggs and veg to turn your broth jelly into an old-school terrine.

Place the water in a bowl, sprinkle over the gelatine and stir until the gelatine is incorporated. Allow to stand for 5 minutes.

Place the broth and gelatine mixture in a saucepan and warm, stirring constantly, over medium–low heat for about 5 minutes, or until completely smooth. Make sure you don't boil the mixture, as the gelatine may not set properly. Season with the salt, pour into ice-cube trays or chocolate moulds and place in the freezer for 15 minutes, or until set.

Once the jellies have set, remove from the trays or moulds and store in an airtight container in the fridge for 2 weeks.

VARIATIONS

For turmeric, cumin and lemon bone broth jellies, add 1 teaspoon lemon juice, ¼ teaspoon ground turmeric and a pinch of ground cumin to the broth and gelatine in the pan.

For turmeric, ginger and cayenne pepper bone broth jellies, add ¼ teaspoon ground turmeric, ¼ teaspoon ground ginger and a pinch of cayenne pepper to the broth and gelatine in the pan.

COCONUT YOGHURT POTS WITH FRESH BERRIES

SERVES 4

3 tablespoons filtered water

1 tablespoon powdered gelatine

3 x 400 ml cans (1.2 litres) coconut cream

1 vanilla pod, split and seeds scraped (optional)

1–2 tablespoons honey, maple syrup or coconut sugar

4 probiotic capsules* or ¼ teaspoon vegetable starter culture*

1 tablespoon lemon juice (optional)

TO SERVE

50 g fresh blueberries

100 g fresh strawberries

50 g fresh raspberries

fresh mint leaves, some finely chopped and some left whole

* See Glossary

Coconut yoghurt is pretty perfect: it's low in carbs and high in fat, plus it contains some wonderful probiotic goodness. Add to that the delicious creamy taste and it gets a double thumbs-up from me. This recipe is super easy to make and you can flavour it with any spices that you love, such as vanilla, cinnamon or ginger.

You'll need a 1.5 litre preserving jar with a lid for this recipe. Wash the jar and all utensils thoroughly in very hot water or run them through a hot rinse cycle in the dishwasher.

Place 3 tablespoons of filtered water in a small bowl, sprinkle over the gelatine and soak for 2 minutes.

Place the coconut milk and vanilla seeds (if using) in a saucepan and gently heat, stirring with a spoon, over medium–low heat until just starting to simmer (90°C, if testing with a thermometer). Do not allow to boil. Immediately remove the pan from the heat. While still hot, mix in the gelatine mixture, then add the sweetener and mix well. Cover the pan with a lid and set aside to cool to lukewarm (35°C or less).

Pour 125 ml of the cooled coconut milk mixture into a sterilised bowl. Open the probiotic capsules (if using). Stir the probiotic powder or starter culture and lemon juice (if using) into the coconut milk in the bowl. Add the remaining coconut milk and mix well.

Pour the coconut milk mixture into the sterilised jar and loosely seal the lid. Ferment in a warm spot for 12 hours at 38–40°C. To maintain this temperature and allow the yoghurt to culture, wrap the jar in a tea towel and place it on a plate in the oven with the door shut and the oven light on. The light's warmth will keep the temperature consistent. Alternatively, place the tea-towel wrapped jar in an esky, fill a heatproof container with boiling water and place it beside the jar – do not allow them to touch – and close the lid. Replace the boiling water halfway through the fermenting process.

Once fermented, the yoghurt tends to form air bubbles and looks as though it has separated. Stir well and refrigerate for at least 5 hours before eating. If it separates after chilling, give it a good whisk. This recipe will yield 1.3 litres. Store it in the fridge for up to 2 weeks.

To serve, divide 400 g of the yoghurt among four ramekins, cups or serving bowls. Top with the fresh berries and garnish with mint.

NOTES
Taste the yoghurt after 12 hours. If you prefer a tangier taste, you can leave it to ferment for another couple of hours. Note that natural sweetener is fine in this recipe as it is needed for the fermentation process. The bacteria fermenting the coconut milk consume the sugar, not you.

2

SOUPS

BROTH WITH GREENS AND BONE MARROW

SERVES 4

800 g centre-cut beef marrow
  bones, cut into 4 cm pieces,
  tendons trimmed (ask your
  butcher to do this)
sea salt
1 litre (4 cups) Chicken, Beef or
  Fish Bone Broth (pages 284, 282
  and 287)
½ onion, sliced
3 silverbeet leaves, chopped
3 rainbow chard leaves, chopped
freshly ground black pepper
1–2 tablespoons lemon juice
1–2 pinches of chilli flakes
  (optional)

This is a very satisfying meal to consume at any time of day or night, and it's one I believe you will start to long for. On most days, our family has ½–1 cup of good-quality bone broth in some form, whether it be straight up, in a soup or as a base for a braise or curry. If you want good fats with low-carb greens or veg, then it doesn't get any easier than this. I really enjoy the addition of bone marrow, as it gives this dish some lovely healthy fat, which is so good for us.

Preheat the oven to 200°C.

Place the marrow bones on a baking tray and season with salt. Roast for 15 minutes until golden brown and cooked through.

Meanwhile, place the broth in a saucepan and bring to a simmer over medium heat. Add the onion and simmer for 5 minutes until tender. Add the silverbeet and chard and cook for 5–8 minutes until softened. Season with salt and pepper.

Scoop the marrow from the roasted bones and add to the broth, then gently stir in the lemon juice to taste.

Ladle the broth into serving bowls and serve with some chilli flakes sprinkled on top, if you like a little heat.

TIP
If rainbow chard is unavailable, you can use kale, but discard the tough stems first.

FISH PHO

SERVES 6

2 onions, one halved and
    one thinly sliced
1 celery stalk, roughly chopped
1 carrot, roughly chopped
70 g ginger, sliced
½ garlic bulb
2 kg fish heads and carcasses
    (such as snapper or
    blue-eye trevalla)
2 pieces of cassia bark or
    2 cinnamon sticks
1 tablespoon coriander seeds
1 tablespoon fennel seeds
6 star anise
6 cardamom pods, bruised
8 cloves
3 ½ tablespoons fish sauce,
    plus extra to taste
2 baby bok choy, trimmed
    and halved
600 g white fish fillet, skin on or off,
    cut into large pieces
320 g daikon, peeled and spiralised
    into thin noodles or sliced into
    thin strips using a mandoline
sea salt

TO SERVE

1 large handful each of mint,
    coriander, Thai basil and
    Vietnamese mint leaves
2 long red chillies, deseeded
    and chopped
lime wedges

If we choose to eat meat for good health, it is imperative that we source meat from animals that have been raised ethically and free from cruelty, and we need to be respectful and grateful and eat nose to tail, not just the expensive cuts. That is where bone broths and soups work so well, as we are generally using the off-cuts or scraps to create a meal. Give this one a go and you will be amazed at how simple it is to create something so nutritious and flavoursome.

Place the onion halves, celery, carrot, ginger and garlic in a stockpot. Add the fish heads, carcasses and spices, then pour in 4 litres of water and place over low heat. Bring to a simmer, frequently skimming any scum from the surface, and cook for 4 hours until fragrant and well flavoured. Stir through the fish sauce and remove from the heat. Allow to cool slightly, then strain the broth into a large bowl or jug. Discard the fish bones and vegetable pulp.

Return the broth to the pot, add the sliced onion and bring to the boil. Reduce the heat to medium–low, add the bok choy and fish and simmer for 1–2 minutes until the fish is just cooked through. Add the daikon noodles and cook for 1–2 minutes until just tender. Season to taste with more fish sauce or some salt.

Fill serving bowls with the daikon noodles, bok choy and fish, then top with the hot broth, herbs and chilli. Serve with lime wedges on the side to squeeze over the pho.

TIP
Always try to source local, sustainable seafood if you can. If you buy a whole fish for this recipe, you can use the head and frame for the broth and then the fillet and offal for the rest of the dish.

MISO SOUP WITH SARDINES

SERVES 4

1 litre (4 cups) Fish or Chicken
   Bone Broth (pages 287 and 284)
2 tablespoons dried wakame*
200 g cauliflower, roughly chopped
6 shiitake mushrooms, sliced
100 g daikon, cut into 1 cm pieces
2 spring onions, thinly sliced
6 fresh okra pods, trimmed
   and roughly chopped
90 g (⅓ cup) miso paste
200 g canned sardines in olive oil
   or brine (or fresh sardine fillets)

TO SERVE
toasted sesame seeds
sesame oil
bonito flakes*

* See Glossary

You may wish to eliminate all soy products, including tamari or miso, if you have an issue with them. I tend to eat a very small amount, but always make sure it is 100 per cent organic and fermented. If you are fine with including miso in your diet, this could well be a winner with your family, as it teams sardines, one of the best seafoods in the world, with a lovely broth. And if sardines are not up your alley, then you can swap them for prawns, clams, mussels, other fish or even pork or chicken.

Bring the broth to the boil in a saucepan over medium heat. Add the wakame and simmer for 10 minutes until the wakame has expanded. Add the vegetables and cook for 5 minutes until tender. Add the miso to the soup – the best way to do this is to push it through a strainer into the pan (this evenly distributes it in the broth). Simmer for 1–2 minutes until the miso has dissolved, stirring gently if needed. Add the sardines and cook for 20 seconds until they are warmed through.

To serve, spoon the soup into warm serving bowls, scatter over some sesame seeds, add 1–2 drops of sesame oil, then sprinkle on some bonito flakes.

TIP
Shichimi togarashi is awesome sprinkled over this dish too.

CHICKEN BROTH WITH SPINACH AND LEMON

SERVES 4

1 litre (4 cups) Chicken Bone Broth
   (page 284)
½ onion, chopped
4 garlic cloves, chopped
150 g English spinach, leaves only,
   roughly chopped
1 large handful of flat-leaf parsley
   leaves, plus extra sprigs to serve
sea salt and freshly ground
   black pepper
1 tablespoon lemon juice
1 teaspoon finely grated lemon zest
extra-virgin olive oil, to serve

This is the perfect dish to include in your diet, especially if you are considering doing a fast. I have added spinach to this recipe, but by all means stick to a classic chicken broth if you prefer. I sometimes like to heat up my broth and add a particular in-season vegetable and cook it until tender, then blend it to create a wonderful soup. Some ingredients you might like to try are mushrooms, broccoli, zucchini, cauliflower, okra, asparagus, onion, Jerusalem artichoke, parsnip and sweet potato (just go easy on the starchy veg if you want to stay low carb).

Bring the broth to the boil in a large saucepan over medium–high heat. Reduce the heat to low, add the onion and garlic and simmer for 15 minutes until the onion is tender. Add the spinach and parsley and cook for 2 minutes.

Using a hand-held blender, blend the soup until smooth. Season with salt and pepper and stir through the lemon juice.

Ladle the soup into serving bowls, sprinkle the lemon zest over the top and drizzle over some olive oil. Garnish with an extra sprig of parsley and serve.

TIP
You can use chopped baby spinach, silverbeet or frozen spinach instead of English spinach.

CHICKEN AND ZUCCHINI NOODLE SOUP WITH AROMATIC SPICES

SERVES 4

2 litres (8 cups) Chicken Bone Broth (page 284)

2 lemongrass stems, pale part only, thinly sliced

2 cinnamon sticks

2 tablespoons finely grated ginger

4 chicken thighs, skin on

1 tablespoon coconut oil or good-quality animal fat*

4 red Asian shallots, sliced

½ teaspoon ground turmeric

3 garlic cloves, sliced

1 spring onion, sliced

8 shiitake mushrooms, sliced

2 choy sum, trimmed and leaves separated

300 g zucchini, spiralised into noodles

4 hard-boiled eggs, halved

SPICE MIX SEASONING

1 small dried chilli

1 teaspoon black peppercorns

1 ½ teaspoons coriander seeds

1 ½ teaspoons cumin seeds

2 teaspoons sea salt

* See Glossary

An oldie but a goodie, the classic chicken noodle soup cannot be beaten ... unless you replace the gluten-containing, carb-loaded noodles with vegetable noodles to make it a win-win for everyone. The flavour is better, your health will ultimately be better and you are getting the nourishing goodness of a wonderful broth that has gelatine, collagen, calcium, glucosamine, magnesium and a host of other benefits just waiting to be slurped up by the whole family. Make sure you cook up a huge batch so you can pack some in a thermos for a beautiful hot lunch.

Place the broth in a saucepan and bring to the boil. Add the lemongrass, cinnamon, ginger and chicken. Bring back to the boil, reduce the heat to medium–low and simmer for 5 minutes. Turn off the heat, cover with the lid and leave the chicken to poach for 45–50 minutes, or until the chicken is cooked through. Carefully remove the chicken from the broth and, when cool enough to handle, remove and discard the bones. Set the broth and chicken aside, keeping warm. Skim any oil that rises to the top of the broth and reserve for cooking.

Meanwhile, to make the spice mix seasoning, toast the chilli, peppercorns, coriander seeds and cumin seeds in a saucepan for 15–20 seconds until fragrant. Remove from the heat and allow to cool. Finely grind the spices using a mortar and pestle or a spice grinder. Transfer to a small bowl, then mix in the salt. Set aside.

Heat the oil or fat in a frying pan over medium heat. Add the shallot and cook for 5 minutes until softened. Add the turmeric, garlic, spring onion and shiitake and sauté for 2 minutes until softened.

Stir the sautéed shallot and mushroom mixture into the broth, add 1 tablespoon of the spice mix seasoning, stir and bring to a simmer. Add the choy sum and simmer for 3 minutes until tender. Season with salt, if needed.

To serve, divide the zucchini noodles among serving bowls. Slice the chicken and arrange on top of the noodles, then add the choy sum and ladle the hot broth over the top. To finish, add two eggs halves to each bowl and sprinkle over the remaining spice mix seasoning.

HEALING CHICKEN BROTH WITH LIVER

SERVES 2–4

700 ml Chicken Bone Broth
  (page 284)
100 g chicken livers, trimmed
  and finely chopped
1 teaspoon ras el hanout (see Note)
sea salt and freshly ground
  black pepper
1 teaspoon finely chopped
  flat-leaf parsley leaves

If you ever want to know what a superfood is, then head straight to the offal section at the butcher or fishmonger and grab yourself some liver (chicken, duck, beef, lamb, pork, venison, kangaroo or fish). Liver is hands-down the greatest superfood on the planet – and you can cook it in so many different ways. When you want true nourishment, add some liver to your broth, as we've done here. (I eat liver a few times a week ... every week!)

Place the broth in a saucepan and bring to a simmer over medium heat. Add the chicken liver and ras el hanout, gently stir to combine and cook for 30 seconds until the liver is just cooked through. Season with salt and pepper.

Pour the hot broth and liver into mugs and sprinkle with the chopped parsley. Take a sip and enjoy.

NOTE
Ras el hanout is a North African spice mix that consists of more than 12 spices. I like to use Herbie's Spices ras el hanout in this recipe. It can be bought from supermarkets, grocers, delis, health-food stores or online. If you can't source ras el hanout, use ground turmeric or ground cumin or a mix of both.

CHINESE EGG DROP SOUP

SERVES 4

1 litre Chicken Bone Broth
  (page 284)
2 chicken thighs
4 cm piece of ginger,
  finely julienned
2 spring onions, sliced, white and
  green parts separated
2 teaspoons tamari or
  coconut aminos*, or to taste
2 eggs, lightly beaten
sea salt and freshly ground
  black pepper
1 teaspoon toasted sesame seeds,
  to serve
sesame oil, to serve

* See Glossary

The Chinese are masters of the broth, in my humble opinion, as their appreciation for the flavour that can be developed through the simple art of simmering animal bones is second to none. You only have to look at the way they use broths in so much of their cooking to appreciate the passion there. Here is my nod to that passion – a delicious chicken broth soup that has the obligatory egg whisked in, along with some spring onions for good measure. Feel free to make this glorious broth your own by adding, subtracting or substituting anything that you love.

Bring the chicken broth to a simmer in a saucepan over medium heat. Add the chicken, ginger, spring onion whites and tamari or coconut aminos and cook for 15 minutes, or until the chicken is cooked through. Remove the chicken thighs from the broth and, when cool enough to handle, shred into pieces.

Return the chicken to the broth, bring to a simmer and then slowly pour in the beaten egg while stirring in one direction. Simmer for a further 30 seconds. Season with salt and pepper, if needed.

To serve, ladle the soup into bowls, sprinkle with the spring onion greens and toasted sesame seeds and drizzle over a little sesame oil.

CHINESE CABBAGE AND PORK MINCE SOUP

SERVES 4

1.25 litres (5 cups) Chicken Bone
  Broth (page 284)
3 spring onions, thinly sliced,
  white and green parts separated
1 large carrot, cut into 1 cm pieces
5 cm piece of ginger, cut into
  matchsticks
200 g Chinese cabbage (wong bok),
  cut into 2.5 cm pieces
½ bunch of Chinese broccoli
  (gai larn) (about 130 g), trimmed
  and chopped into 2.5 cm pieces
1 teaspoon tamari or coconut
  aminos*, plus extra if needed
1 teaspoon fish sauce, plus extra
  if needed

SEASONED PORK MINCE

400 g pork mince
½ teaspoon freshly ground
  white pepper
2 tablespoons tamari or
  coconut aminos*
1 teaspoon fish sauce
1 teaspoon sesame oil

* See Glossary

Nothing nourishes our bodies in the cooler months like an intoxicating bowl of steaming broth. These flavoursome soups have been with us ever since we learned how to use animals' shells and hides as vessels for cooking bones and water with whatever else we could gather to add for goodness. And, when you look at a dish like this, you can see that not a lot has changed over the tens of thousands of years. Play around with different types of mince, vegetables and seasonings if you like to mix things up, or simply follow this recipe to a T for a culinary taste adventure.

To make the seasoned pork mince, combine the pork, white pepper, tamari or coconut aminos, fish sauce and sesame oil in a bowl and mix thoroughly. Set aside.

Place half the broth in a large saucepan and bring to a simmer. Add the white part of the spring onion, the carrot and ginger and cook for 5 minutes. Add the seasoned pork mince and break up the mince with a wooden spoon to form bite-sized pieces. Pour in the remaining broth, cover with the lid and simmer for 5 minutes until the mince is almost cooked through.

Add the Chinese cabbage and Chinese broccoli to the pan, then stir in the tamari or coconut aminos and the fish sauce. Cook for 5 minutes until the vegetables have softened and the mince is cooked through. Taste the soup and add a little splash of extra tamari or coconut aminos and fish sauce if needed. To finish, sprinkle with the remaining spring onion and serve.

VIETNAMESE BEEF NOODLE SOUP (BUN BO HUE)

SERVES 6–8

3 kg beef bones

2 onions, one halved and one
  thinly sliced

2 lemongrass stems, pale part only,
  bruised

¼ pineapple (about 230 g), chopped

4 kaffir lime leaves

sea salt

700 g pork belly

700 g oyster blade steak or beef brisket

3 tablespoons lime juice

1 tablespoon fish sauce, plus extra
  if needed

1 tablespoon coconut sugar,
  plus extra if needed

1 kg beef marrow bones, cut into 3 cm
  pieces (ask your butcher to do this)

freshly ground black pepper

CHILLI PASTE

80 ml (⅓ cup) coconut oil

6 garlic cloves, peeled

3 red Asian shallots, peeled

2 lemongrass stems, pale part only,
  chopped

1 tablespoon chilli powder

1 tablespoon shrimp paste

TO SERVE

4 zucchini, spiralised into thick
  noodles or sliced into long, thin
  strips using a mandoline

250 g Chinese cabbage (wong bok),
  finely shredded

1 large handful of mixed herbs
  (such as coriander, Thai basil,
  Vietnamese mint and mint)

2 long red chillies, thinly sliced
  (optional)

2 spring onions, thinly sliced

lime wedges

By retaining the beef (bo) and eliminating the rice noodles (bun), I have turned this popular classic from the Vietnamese city of Hue into a low-carb dish. Using zucchini rather than rice noodles makes this broth more nutrient dense and faster to prepare – the zucchini noodles take only 1 minute to cook!

Preheat the oven to 200°C.

To make the chilli paste, place all the ingredients in the bowl of a food processor and process to a thick, fine paste.

Heat a frying pan over medium–low heat, add the chilli paste and fry, stirring frequently (so the spices don't burn), for 5 minutes until fragrant and the oil separates. Remove from the heat and set aside.

Place the beef bones on a baking tray and roast for 30–40 minutes until well browned. Transfer the bones to a stockpot, add the onion halves, lemongrass, pineapple, lime leaves and 1 tablespoon of salt and cover with 5 litres of water. Bring to the boil, skimming off any scum that rises to the top. Turn down the heat to medium–low, add the pork belly and oyster blade or brisket and simmer for 2½–3 hours until the pork belly is soft and tender. Carefully remove the pork belly from the broth, place it on a plate, cover and set aside to cool. When cool, transfer to the fridge. Continue to cook the oyster blade or brisket in the broth for 1½–2 hours until soft and tender. Remove the beef from the broth, place on a plate, cover and set aside.

Strain the stock (discard the leftover bones and vegetable pulp), then return to the pot and place over medium heat. Add the sliced onion and cook for 10 minutes until the onion has softened.

Remove the pork from the fridge. Cut the pork and beef into bite-sized pieces, add to the broth and simmer for 5 minutes. Add the chilli paste and stir well. Mix in the lime juice and season with the fish sauce and coconut sugar, adding more to taste if you wish.

Meanwhile, preheat the oven to 200°C.

Season the bone marrow flesh with salt and pepper, place on a baking tray and roast in the oven for 15 minutes until cooked through and starting to brown. Remove from the oven and keep warm.

Fill each serving bowl with some zucchini noodles and pork belly and beef, top with the cabbage, broth, herbs, roasted bone marrow, chilli (if using) and spring onion. Serve with the lime wedges on the side.

BEEF BROTH WITH TURMERIC, COCONUT CREAM AND GINGER

SERVES 3

500 ml (2 cups) Beef Bone Broth
   (page 282)
1 tablespoon finely grated ginger
½ teaspoon ground turmeric,
   plus extra to serve
250 ml (1 cup) coconut cream
sea salt and freshly ground
   black pepper
juice of ½ lime (optional)
1 teaspoon finely chopped
   coriander leaves

If you have read any of my other books, you will know by now how important bone broth is for your gut and overall health. This simple beef broth comes in handy when you want something in the morning to get you through to lunchtime or when you don't want a full meal at the end of the day. For variation, you could easily replace the beef base with chicken, pork or fish, then add in the ginger, turmeric and coconut cream (make sure it is full fat) and I guarantee you will feel wonderfully satiated. If you need or want extra fat, then add in some coconut oil or bone marrow.

Place the broth, ginger, turmeric and coconut cream in a saucepan and bring to a simmer over medium heat. Cook, stirring occasionally, for 5 minutes to allow the ginger and turmeric to infuse. Season with salt and pepper. If you like your broth slightly sour, stir through the lime juice to taste.

Pour the broth into mugs, sprinkle on the coriander and a touch more turmeric, take a sip and enjoy!

TIP
If you can source fresh organic turmeric, then grate some of that to use instead of the powdered form.

3

MAIN MEALS

SAVOURY GRANOLA BREAKFAST BOWL

SERVES 2

4 eggs

1 tablespoon coconut cream
or almond milk

sea salt and freshly ground
black pepper

1 tablespoon coconut oil or
good-quality animal fat*

1 handful of baby spinach leaves

2 radishes, thinly sliced

1 small handful of alfalfa sprouts

4 tablespoons Sauerkraut
(page 295), plus 2 tablespoons
sauerkraut juice

½ avocado, halved lengthways

1 tablespoon extra-virgin olive oil,
avocado oil or macadamia oil

SAVOURY GRANOLA

70 g (½ cup) pumpkin seeds
(activated if possible*)

70 g sunflower seeds
(activated if possible*)

3 tablespoons sesame seeds

40 g (¾ cup) coconut flakes

1–2 teaspoons currants (optional)

¾ teaspoon sea salt

2 teaspoons ground turmeric

1 teaspoon ground cumin

1 teaspoon curry powder

½ teaspoon ground cinnamon

pinch of cayenne pepper

3 ½ tablespoons flaxseeds,
soaked in 3 tablespoons water
for 5 minutes

1 ½ tablespoons coconut oil, melted

1 teaspoon honey or maple syrup
(optional)

* See Glossary

You will love the flavour and texture of this amazing granola.
I reckon it will become one of your favourite meals. My advice is
to make a large batch and, when it has cooled, keep it in an airtight
container so you can serve it, as I have done here, with eggs and
a salad or add it to curries, stir-fries, cooked veggies or grilled
fish and meat. And if you want to change things up, please play
around with different spice combinations.

Preheat the oven to 160°C. Line a baking tray with baking paper.

To make the granola, place all the ingredients in a bowl and mix well
to combine. Pour the mixture onto the lined tray and spread out
evenly. Bake, stirring a few times to ensure it cooks evenly, for
20 minutes until lightly golden. Allow to cool completely before
serving or transferring to a storage container.

Whisk the eggs and coconut cream or almond milk in a bowl and
season with salt and pepper.

Melt the coconut oil or fat in a non-stick frying pan over medium
heat, pour in the egg mixture and stir gently with a wooden spoon for
2 ½–3 ½ minutes until the egg sets.

Divide the scrambled eggs between serving bowls, add 3–4 spoonfuls
of granola, the spinach leaves, radish, alfalfa sprouts, sauerkraut
and avocado, then drizzle the sauerkraut juice and olive, avocado
or macadamia oil over the salad and serve.

TIP

Store any leftover granola in an airtight container in the fridge
for up to 3 months.

STIR-FRY VEGGIE OMELETTE

SERVES 2

3 tablespoons coconut oil or
good-quality animal fat*

¼ onion, chopped

130 g broccoli, cut into florets

1 carrot, sliced on an angle

1 spring onion, cut into 4 cm batons,
white and green parts separated

80 g mushrooms, sliced

¼ zucchini, sliced on an angle

1 teaspoon finely grated ginger

2 garlic cloves, thinly sliced

80 g Chinese cabbage, chopped

1 tablespoon tamari or
coconut aminos*

1 teaspoon sesame seeds

sea salt and freshly ground
black pepper

6 eggs

a few sprigs of coriander, to serve

* See Glossary

Who doesn't love a stir-fry of delicious vegetables? To make it even more delicious, try popping them in an omelette so you have an amazing breakfast, lunch or dinner for when you want to up your veggie intake. Of course, you could also add some meat of your choice to this, such as sausages, prawns, chicken or duck, to take it to a whole other level.

To make the stir-fried veggies, heat 2 tablespoons of oil or fat in a wok over medium–high heat. Add the onion and cook for 5 minutes until softened. Add the broccoli, carrot and white parts of the spring onion and sauté for 4 minutes, stirring frequently. Add the mushrooms, zucchini, ginger and garlic and cook for 2 minutes, then add the Chinese cabbage and cook for 1 minute. Pour in the tamari or coconut aminos, mix through the sesame seeds and season with salt and pepper. Set the stir-fried veggies aside while you prepare the omelettes.

To make the omelettes, crack the eggs into a bowl and whisk lightly until combined. Season with a pinch of salt and pepper.

Heat one teaspoon of the oil or fat in a frying pan over medium heat. Pour in half of the egg mixture and tilt the pan so the mixture covers the base. Cook for 1 minute until the omelette is set underneath and just set top. Slide onto a plate and repeat the process to make the second omelette.

Spoon the stir-fried veggies on top of each omelette, garnish with the coriander sprigs and serve.

GREEN OMELETTE WITH OVEN-BAKED TOMATO, MUSHROOMS AND BACON

SERVES 2

100 g button mushrooms or any
    mushrooms of your choice
    (such as field, portobello or Swiss)
1 truss tomato, halved
2 tablespoons coconut oil or
    good-quality animal fat*, melted
4 thyme sprigs
sea salt and freshly ground
    black pepper
120 g (2 cups) baby spinach leaves
    or 100 g (½ cup) thawed frozen
    spinach
4 eggs
2 tablespoons coconut cream
4 rindless bacon rashers
1–2 tablespoons fermented
    vegetables of your choice
    (optional)

* See Glossary

It would be cliché of me to talk about Dr Seuss here, so I will anyway. *Green Eggs and Ham* was one of my all-time favourite books as a kid (well, any of the good doctor's books were, to be honest). I just love this play on the classic story and I reckon the kids will love it too. I have teamed my eggs with the usual suspects of bacon, mushrooms and tomato, but feel free to serve yours with ham or any other ingredients you have on hand.

Preheat the oven to 180°C.

Place the mushrooms and tomato halves on a baking tray and drizzle with 1 tablespoon of oil or fat. Sprinkle over the thyme and season with salt and pepper. Roast for 10–15 minutes until the mushrooms are lightly golden and cooked through and the tomatoes are soft and juicy.

Bring a saucepan of lightly salted water to the boil. Add the baby spinach and cook for 10 seconds, then drain immediately and plunge into ice-cold water to stop the cooking process. Drain again, then place in a clean tea towel and squeeze out the excess liquid. If using thawed frozen spinach, simply squeeze out all the excess water.

Pop the spinach into the jug of a high-speed blender, crack in the eggs, then add the coconut cream and blend until smooth. Season with salt and pepper. Set aside.

Heat a chargrill pan over high heat and grill the bacon for 2 minutes on each side until charred. Alternatively, heat a frying pan over medium–high heat and cook the bacon on each side for 2 minutes until golden or cooked to your liking. Set aside, keeping warm.

To make the omelette, melt 2 teaspoons of the remaining oil or fat in a non-stick frying pan over medium–high heat and swirl around the pan. Pour in half the green egg mixture and tilt the pan so the omelette mixture covers the base. Cook for 1–2 minutes until set on the underside and still slightly runny on top. Flip the omelette over and cook for a further 15–20 seconds until just cooked through. Slide the omelette onto a plate and repeat this process with the remaining omelette mixture.

To serve, place an omelette on each serving plate, then add a roasted tomato half, the mushrooms, grilled bacon and thyme. Add the fermented vegetables (if desired) and serve.

MUSHROOM OMELETTE WITH SILVERBEET

SERVES 2

2 ½ tablespoons coconut oil or
    good-quality animal fat*
½ onion, finely chopped
6 field mushrooms, sliced
2 garlic cloves, finely chopped
1 tablespoon chopped flat-leaf
    parsley leaves
1 tablespoon chopped basil leaves
sea salt and freshly ground
    black pepper
6 eggs
2 silverbeet leaves, stems removed
    and leaves torn (keep the stems
    for broths)
Sauerkraut (page 295), to serve

* See Glossary

I recall learning how to make omelettes at culinary school. The secret to the best omelette is to start with great organic free-range eggs, then to cook them gently in a good amount of fat in a top-quality pan. Season the eggs very well and add in your favourite ingredients. My kids love ham and chive omelettes, whereas I enjoy prawns and coriander topped with avocado and hot sauce.

That said, you really can't go past a good mushroom omelette when mushrooms are abundant and in season. This makes for a great lunch for work or school.

Melt 1 tablespoon of oil or fat in a frying pan over medium heat. Add the onion and cook for 4–5 minutes until translucent. Add the mushrooms and cook, tossing occasionally, for 2 minutes until lightly browned and softened. Stir in the garlic and cook for 1 minute, then toss through the herbs and season with salt and pepper. Remove from the pan and keep warm.

To make the omelettes, crack the eggs into a bowl and whisk lightly until combined. Season with a pinch of salt and pepper. Wipe the pan clean and place over medium heat. Heat 1 teaspoon of oil or fat in the pan. Pour in half the egg mixture and tilt the pan so the mixture covers the base. Cook for 1 minute, or until the egg is set on the underside and still runny on top. Spoon half the cooked mushroom mixture onto half of the omelette and cook for 1–2 minutes until the egg is lightly golden on the underside and just set on top. Fold the uncovered half of the omelette over the mushroom mixture, slide onto a serving plate and keep warm. Repeat this process to make the second omelette.

Wipe the pan clean and place over medium–high heat. Heat the remaining oil or fat in the pan, then add the silverbeet and 3 tablespoons of water. Cook, tossing occasionally, for 4 minutes until the silverbeet is wilted. Season with a little salt and pepper, if desired. Divide the silverbeet between the plates and serve with the sauerkraut on the side.

CAULIFLOWER AND BACON TOAST WITH AVOCADO AND FRIED EGG

SERVES 4

1 ½ tablespoons coconut oil or
    good-quality animal fat*
4 eggs
1 avocado, sliced
Chilli Oil (page 285), to serve
1 handful of watercress
pinch of chilli flakes (optional)
1 lemon, cut into wedges

CAULIFLOWER AND BACON TOAST

¼ head of cauliflower (about 300 g),
    chopped into small pieces
1 ½ tablespoons coconut oil
sea salt and freshly ground
    black pepper
2 rindless bacon rashers
    (about 100 g), finely diced
2 eggs

* See Glossary

The whole premise of this book is to get you eating less carbs, but that does not mean we want to deprive you of flavour or enjoyment. I have tried to emulate some favourite dishes so you can still eat the foods you have grown to love. This cauliflower and bacon toast recipe is super simple and will make missing bread a thing of the past. We have teamed the cauliflower toast with egg and avo, which makes for a perfect meal any time.

Preheat the oven to 200°C. Line a baking tray with baking paper.

To make the cauliflower and bacon toast, place the cauliflower in the bowl of a food processor and process to fine crumbs. Melt 1 tablespoon of coconut oil in a large frying pan over medium heat. Add the cauliflower crumbs and cook for 4–6 minutes until softened. Season with salt and pepper, transfer to a large bowl and allow to cool. Wipe the pan clean, add the remaining oil and fry the bacon over medium–high heat for about 3–4 minutes until lightly golden. Allow to cool. Add the cooled bacon to the cauliflower, crack in the eggs and mix to combine. Season with salt and pepper. Spoon 2 tablespoons of the cauliflower mixture onto the prepared tray and gently spread out to form a patty, approximately 8 cm in diameter. Repeat, allowing 2 cm between each patty, until all the mixture is used and you have four patties in total. Bake for 15–20 minutes until golden and crisp.

Heat the oil or fat in a frying pan over medium heat. Crack the eggs into the pan (if the pan is not big enough to cook all the eggs at once, it's best to cook them in batches). Cook the eggs for 2 ½–3 minutes or to your liking. Season with salt and pepper.

To serve, transfer the cauliflower and bacon toast patties to a platter or serving plates, add a few slices of avocado to each, then slide an egg on top. Drizzle with a little chilli oil, sprinkle on a few sprigs of watercress, add some chilli flakes, if desired, and serve with the lemon wedges on the side.

SPICED EGG CURRY

SERVES 4

2 tablespoons coconut oil or
   good-quality animal fat*
1 onion, chopped
4 garlic cloves, finely chopped
1 tablespoon finely grated ginger
1 tablespoon ground coriander
1 tablespoon ground cumin
2 teaspoons ground turmeric
2 teaspoons garam masala
2 pinches of cayenne pepper
   (add more if you like it spicy!)
1 × 400 g can whole peeled
   tomatoes, crushed
1 × 400 ml can coconut cream
125 ml (½ cup) Chicken Bone Broth
   (page 284) or water
sea salt and freshly ground
   black pepper
8 hard-boiled eggs, peeled
   and halved

SALAD
1 large handful of watercress
1 large handful of coriander leaves
1 teaspoon extra-virgin olive oil

TO SERVE
Broccoli or Cauliflower Rice
   (page 283) (optional)
lemon wedges

* See Glossary

We are lucky enough to have our own chickens that lay the most beautiful eggs for us, so we are always looking for ways to make them shine. If you want to create a protein-rich dish full of healthy fat for breakfast, lunch or even dinner, then look no further than this quick egg curry. You can also add prawns, chicken or any vegetables that you have.

Melt the oil or fat in a large saucepan over medium heat. Add the onion and sauté for 5 minutes until translucent. Add the garlic and ginger and cook for 1 minute, then stir in the spices and sauté for about 30 seconds until fragrant. Pour in the crushed tomatoes, coconut cream and broth or water, stir well and simmer for 20 minutes until the curry sauce thickens. Season with salt and pepper.

Gently place the eggs in the curry sauce and cook for 2–3 minutes until just heated through.

Just before serving, make the salad. Place the watercress and coriander in a bowl, pour over the olive oil and gently toss to combine.

Spoon the egg curry onto serving plates and neatly pile some salad on the side. Serve with hot broccoli or cauliflower rice, if desired, and some wedges of lemon to squeeze over the top.

JAPANESE EGG CUSTARDS WITH PRAWNS (CHAWANMUSHI)

SERVES 4

500 ml (2 cups) Chicken Bone
    Broth (page 284)
sea salt
4 tablespoons bonito flakes*
½ teaspoon finely grated ginger
3 teaspoons tamari or
    coconut aminos*
4 eggs, beaten
2 shiitake mushrooms, sliced
2 spring onions, thinly sliced,
    white and green parts separated
1 bok choy, trimmed and
    leaves separated
4 cooked, chopped king prawns

TO SERVE

1–2 tablespoons salmon roe
2 pinches of Furikake Seasoning
    (page 188)
baby shiso leaves (optional)
Chilli Oil (page 285) (optional)

* See Glossary

Chawanmushi – steamed egg custard with the most luxurious texture and flavour – is a dish I have been making for the past 25 years or so, since I first discovered Japanese cuisine. Typical ingredients include prawns or scampi or other seafoods, such as sea urchin, scallops, crabmeat and mussels. You could also pop in some pork belly, roast chicken or bacon and mushrooms or spring onions. Give this a go for breakfast one day and I promise you will enjoy it. Traditionally a spoon, not chopsticks, is used and it can be eaten hot or cold, which is perfect if you want to make it in advance to enjoy later.

To make the custard, place the broth, ½ teaspoon of salt, bonito flakes, ginger and tamari or coconut aminos in a saucepan. Stir with a wooden spoon, then gently heat until the broth is warmed through and the sugar has dissolved. Remove from the heat and steep for 30 minutes to allow the flavours to develop. (Make sure the mixture is at room temperature before adding the beaten egg, as the custard may curdle.) Carefully add the beaten egg, gently stirring through the cooled broth mixture with a wooden spoon (you don't want any bubbles). Strain through a fine sieve and discard the bonito flakes.

Pour the custard mixture into four small heatproof bowls and fill to about 2.5 cm from the top. Add the shiitake mushrooms and the white part of the spring onion to each bowl, then cover with baking paper. Place in a bamboo steamer over a saucepan of simmering water, cover with the lid and steam for 15–17 minutes until a skewer inserted in the centre of a custard comes out clean. The custards should be just set but still wobbly and moist. Remove the bowls from the steamer.

Add the bok choy to the steamer and steam for 2 minutes until tender. Season with some salt.

Top each custard with the prawns, bok choy and salmon roe. Sprinkle over some furikake seasoning, the spring onion greens and the shiso (if using) and add a drizzle of chilli oil, if you like. Serve hot or cold.

EGGS FLORENTINE WITH BAKED MUSHROOMS

SERVES 4

4 large portobello or field
   mushrooms, stems removed

2 tablespoons coconut oil or
   good-quality animal fat*, melted

sea salt and freshly ground
   black pepper

2 tablespoons apple cider vinegar

4 eggs

2 garlic cloves, finely chopped

150 g baby spinach leaves

120 g Hollandaise Sauce (page 289)

1 teaspoon finely chopped chives

* See Glossary

Hollandaise and béarnaise were two of the first sauces I learned to make at culinary school. And that's because these sauces are the backbone of classic dishes like steak with béarnaise and eggs benedict. These delicious sauces are traditionally made from egg yolks and clarified butter, but you can make them using coconut oil or animal fat, as we have done. Once you have mastered the art of making a hollandaise or béarnaise sauce, you can put them on steamed or grilled fish, grilled steak, asparagus and, of course, eggs. For this recipe, I have replaced the toast or English muffins with mushrooms, but feel free to use paleo bread or cauliflower and bacon toast (page 118) as an option. Oh, and the difference between hollandaise and béarnaise? The béarnaise is flavoured with tarragon and shallot.

Preheat the oven to 200°C.

Place the mushrooms on a baking tray, drizzle over 1 tablespoon of oil or fat and season with salt and pepper. Cover with foil and bake in the oven for 12–15 minutes until cooked through.

Meanwhile, to poach the eggs, pour the vinegar into a saucepan of boiling salted water. Reduce the heat to medium–low so the water is just simmering. Crack an egg into a cup and, using a wooden spoon, stir the simmering water in one direction to form a whirlpool, then drop the egg into the centre. Repeat with the remaining eggs and cook for 3 minutes, or until the eggs are cooked to your liking. Use a slotted spoon to remove the eggs, then place them on paper towel to soak up the excess water.

Heat the remaining oil or fat in a non-stick frying pan over medium–high heat. Add the garlic and sauté for 10 seconds until fragrant, then add the spinach and cook for about 1 minute until the spinach is just wilted. Season with salt and pepper.

Divide the mushrooms among warm serving plates, then top each with the wilted spinach and a poached egg. Spoon over the hollandaise sauce, sprinkle on the chives and a little salt and pepper and serve immediately.

PRAWN COCKTAIL AVO BOWLS

SERVES 2–4

400 g cooked prawn meat, chopped
1 celery stick, cut in half lengthways
    and finely sliced
2 radishes, finely julienned
1 tablespoon chopped chives
1 teaspoon chopped tarragon leaves
sea salt and freshly ground
    black pepper
2 avocados, halved and
    stone removed
4 sprigs of watercress, to serve
lemon cheeks, to serve

COCKTAIL SAUCE

100 g Mayonnaise (page 292)
1 tablespoon Tomato Ketchup
    (page 296)
1 teaspoon Worcestershire Sauce
    (page 297)
4 drops of tabasco sauce

This dish could easily be a quick breakfast, delicious work lunch or an amazing dinner on a hot summer's evening – or how about taking it for a picnic down at the beach? This dish should take no more than 10 minutes to make from start to finish, especially if you have already bought cooked and chilled prawns. If prawns are tricky to come by, simply swap them for some good-quality cooked tuna, salmon, eel, mackerel, sardines, smoked mussels or even some roast chicken or pork.

To make the cocktail sauce, combine all the ingredients in a bowl. Set aside.

To make the prawn salad, combine the prawns, celery, radish, chives, tarragon and half of the cocktail sauce in a bowl. Season with salt and pepper.

Spoon the salad generously into the hollow of each avocado half and garnish with a sprig of watercress. Serve with lemon cheeks and the remaining cocktail sauce on the side.

TIP

You can score the avocado in squares before adding the filling, if you like, to make it easier to scoop out the flesh.

ZUCCHETTI AGLIO E OLIO WITH PRAWNS

SERVES 4

4–5 large zucchini

80 ml (⅓ cup) coconut oil or
    good-quality animal fat*

20 raw king prawns, shelled and
    deveined with tails intact

sea salt and freshly ground
    black pepper

8 garlic cloves, finely chopped

4–5 long red chillies, deseeded
    and finely chopped

4 tablespoons finely chopped
    flat-leaf parsley

6 anchovy fillets, finely chopped

80 ml (⅓ cup) extra-virgin olive oil

2 teaspoons finely grated
    lemon zest

1 tablespoon lemon juice

* See Glossary

Aglio e olio simply translates from the Italian to mean garlic and oil. It is a classic pasta dish that many Italian college students eat as their version of 2-minute noodles. With this recipe, I have replaced the pasta with spiralised zucchini noodles. The whole dish can be on the table in 2–3 minutes, so there really is no excuse to eat those other noodles anymore. Oh, and you don't need to use prawns – you can add bacon, an egg, roast chicken or a jar of salmon, tuna or sardines if you prefer.

Using the thick noodle blade on a spiraliser, spiralise the zucchini into long noodles. If you don't have a spiraliser, use a sharp knife to cut the zucchini lengthways into long thin strips. Set aside until needed.

Melt 2 tablespoons of coconut oil or fat in a large frying pan over medium–high heat. Season the prawns with salt and pepper, add to the pan in batches and cook for 40–60 seconds on each side until just cooked through. Remove from the pan and set aside, covered loosely with foil to keep warm.

Wipe the pan clean and place over medium heat. Add the remaining coconut oil or fat, then add the garlic and chilli and cook for 30 seconds until the garlic starts to colour. Stir in the parsley and cook for 10 seconds to release its flavour. Add the anchovies and cook, stirring, for a further minute. Now, stir in the zucchini spaghetti and sauté for 1½ minutes until the zucchini is almost cooked through. Season with a little salt and pepper and remove from the heat. Add the cooked prawns, olive oil and lemon zest and juice and toss to combine.

SARDINE AND ZUCCHINI FRITTATA WITH WATERCRESS AND RADICCHIO SALAD

SERVES 4

2 tablespoons coconut oil or
    good-quality animal fat*, melted,
    plus extra for greasing
1 onion, finely chopped
1 zucchini, cut on an angle into
    5 mm thick slices
sea salt and freshly ground
    black pepper
8 large eggs
2 silverbeet or chard leaves,
    stems removed and leaves
    roughly chopped (reserve the
    stems for broths)
4 sardine fillets from a jar
1 handful of watercress
½ radicchio, leaves torn
1 teaspoon extra-virgin olive oil
½ teaspoon lemon juice or
    apple cider vinegar
1–2 pinches of chilli flakes
    (optional)

TO SERVE

Fermented Kimchi Mayonnaise or
    Mayonnaise (pages 287 and 292)
lemon wedges

* See Glossary

I know I may not be making many friends with this recipe, but I do like to share the dishes I love to cook and eat. This meal came about recently when I didn't have any protein on hand other than a jar of sardines and some eggs. I thought this combination would make for a pretty amazing omelette and, I gotta say, I wasn't disappointed. It was absolutely delicious – and, best of all, took only a few minutes to whip up. Feel free to change the sardines for wild salmon, mackerel, eel, prawns or even something as simple as leftover cooked chicken or sausage.

Preheat the oven to 220°C.

Heat 1 tablespoon of coconut oil or fat in a frying pan over medium–high heat. Add the onion and cook for about 5–8 minutes until translucent. Remove from the pan and set aside.

Wipe the pan clean, return to medium–high heat and add the remaining coconut oil or fat. Add the zucchini slices in batches and cook on one side for 1 minute until slightly golden, then remove from the pan. Season with salt and pepper and set aside until needed.

Whisk the eggs with a pinch of salt and pepper in a bowl.

Grease an ovenproof frying pan with a little coconut oil or fat. Scatter on the silverbeet or chard and cooked onion in a single layer. Pour over the egg mixture, then arrange the zucchini on top and press down lightly. Cook the frittata over medium heat for 30 seconds, then transfer to the oven for 5 minutes. Remove from the oven, arrange the sardines on the frittata, then return to the oven for 3 minutes until the eggs are lightly golden and the sardines are cooked through. Allow to rest for a minute in the pan, then slide onto a board or plate.

Meanwhile, place the watercress and radicchio in a small bowl, add the olive oil and lemon juice or vinegar and gently toss to combine. Season with a little salt and pepper.

Top the frittata with the watercress and radicchio salad and chilli flakes (if using) and serve with some mayonnaise and lemon wedges on the side.

PAN-FRIED BLUE MACKEREL WITH PICKLED ZUCCHINI AND ALMOND AIOLI

SERVES 4

2 bunches of broccolini
(about 440 g), trimmed
4 × 110 g blue mackerel fillets,
pin-boned
sea salt and freshly ground
black pepper
2 tablespoons coconut oil
or good-quality animal fat*,
plus extra if needed
200 g Pickled Zucchini with
Turmeric (page 197)
1 lemon, cut into cheeks
2 tablespoons extra-virgin olive oil

ALMOND AIOLI
10 almonds (activated if possible*),
toasted and finely chopped
100 g Aioli (page 280)

* See Glossary

We grow zucchini in the summertime on the farm and find ourselves inundated with an excess. I know others who grow their own experience this too and struggle with what to do with so many zucchini. Well, pickling is the answer. If you have never tried pickled zucchini, let me tell you now, it is one of the gastronomic wonders of the world – and so simple to make. Pickled zucchini goes so well with so many dishes: burgers, roasts, curries, egg dishes and, my all-time favourite, some simply grilled fish with or without a little aioli on the side.

Blanch the broccolini in boiling salted water for 2–2 ½ minutes until just tender, then drain well. Set aside, keeping warm.

Meanwhile, season the mackerel with salt. Heat the coconut oil or fat in a frying pan over medium–high heat, add the mackerel, skin-side down, in batches and cook for 1 minute. Turn and cook for 20–30 seconds, then transfer to serving plates.

Return the pan to medium heat, add a little extra coconut oil or fat, if needed, and sauté the broccolini for 30 seconds until hot and starting to slightly colour. Season with salt and pepper.

Next, to make the almond aioli, mix the chopped almonds into the aioli, then spoon onto the plates beside the fish. Divide the broccolini and pickles among the plates, add the lemon cheeks and drizzle on some olive oil to finish.

ZUCCHINI NOODLES WITH TUNA, CHILLI, ROCKET AND CAPERS

SERVES 4

4 large zucchini (about 600 g)

400 g tuna loin, cut into 2 cm dice

2 long red chillies, deseeded and thinly sliced

3 tablespoons salted baby capers, rinsed and drained

2 large handfuls of rocket (about 100 g)

lemon wedges, to serve

DRESSING

1 tablespoon extra-virgin olive oil

2 tablespoons Chilli Oil (page 285)

3 tablespoons Garlic Oil (page 288)

3 tablespoons lemon juice

sea salt and freshly ground black pepper

Oh my goodness is the only explanation needed for this dish! And it takes less than 5 minutes to make from start to finish.

Using the thick noodle blade on a spiraliser, spiralise the zucchini into long noodles. If you don't have a spiraliser, use a sharp knife to cut the zucchini lengthways into long thin strips. Set aside until needed.

To make the dressing, whisk the oils and lemon juice in a bowl and season with salt and pepper. Set aside.

Place the tuna, chilli, capers and rocket in a bowl. Set aside.

Blanch the zucchini noodles in a large saucepan of boiling salted water for 5 seconds until al dente. Drain well.

Toss the zucchini noodles with the tuna mixture and pour over the dressing. Gently mix to combine and serve immediately with the lemon wedges on the side.

SPICY TUNA HAND ROLLS

SERVES 4

100 g (⅓ cup) Mayonnaise
   (page 292)
1 tablespoon Sriracha Chilli Sauce
   (page 296)
½ teaspoon finely grated ginger
200 g canned tuna in brine, drained
200 g (1 cup) cooked and chilled
   Cauliflower Rice (page 283)
4 toasted nori sheets*
1 avocado, sliced
1 Lebanese cucumber,
   cut into matchsticks
½ carrot, cut into matchsticks
1 small handful of baby shiso leaves
   (optional)
1 teaspoon black sesame seeds,
   toasted
1 teaspoon white sesame seeds,
   toasted

TO SERVE
tamari or coconut aminos*
wasabi paste

* See Glossary

We love making nori rolls with the girls. Here, I've suggested an assortment of fillings to play around with. Bind your cauliflower rice with a little mayo, tahini or avo, add good-quality animal protein – such as prawns, chicken, fish (cooked or raw), crab, eel, sea urchin, beef (cooked or raw) or omelette – and veggies and herbs – such as cucumber, avocado, radish, carrot, celery, rocket, lettuce, daikon, okra, asparagus, eggplant, pumpkin, mushrooms, coriander, shiso, wasabi leaf, spring onions, chives, mint or Vietnamese mint, parsley and Thai basil. And don't forget to include some tamari or coconut aminos, sesame seeds, wasabi paste and salmon roe or other caviar and seasonings like togarashi, furikake or gomashio. To finish add some kimchi or kraut. Phew! I reckon that will do it.

Mix the mayonnaise, sriracha chilli sauce and ginger in a serving bowl. Set aside.

Combine the tuna, half the sriracha mayonnaise and the cauliflower rice in a bowl and mix well. Refrigerate for 5 minutes.

Cut each nori sheet in half to form eight 10 cm × 18 cm pieces. Place a nori piece in the palm of your hand, shiny-side down, and top with some of the spicy tuna mixture, followed by the avocado, cucumber, carrot and shiso leaves (if using). Fold the bottom corner of the nori over the filling, and then roll up to form a cone shape. Repeat to make eight rolls.

Dollop a teaspoon of the reserved sriracha mayonnaise onto the filling and sprinkle on the sesame seeds. Serve immediately with the tamari or coconut aminos as a dipping sauce and the wasabi on the side.

TUNA POKE WITH FRIED EGG AND COCONUT TORTILLA

SERVES 4

1 ½ avocados, diced

1 ½ tablespoons lime juice

1 tablespoon extra-virgin olive oil

freshly ground black pepper

2 tablespoons coconut oil or
 good-quality animal fat*

4 eggs

1 Lebanese cucumber, deseeded
 and cut into matchsticks

350 g sashimi-grade tuna,
 cut into small dice

1 lime, cut into wedges

coriander leaves, to serve

POKE DRESSING

½ French shallot, finely chopped

1 garlic clove, finely grated

1 spring onion, green part
 thinly sliced and white part
 finely chopped

½ long red chilli, thinly sliced, or
 ½ teaspoon chilli flakes (add more
 if you like it spicy) (optional)

1 teaspoon finely grated ginger

2 tablespoons tamari or
 coconut aminos*

2 teaspoons sesame oil

2 tablespoons extra-virgin olive oil

1 teaspoon toasted black and white
 sesame seeds, plus extra to serve

COCONUT TORTILLA

100 g (1 cup) almond meal

125 g (1 cup) tapioca flour*

125 ml (½ cup) coconut milk

1 egg

sea salt

coconut oil, for cooking

* See Glossary

Poke (pronounced 'pokey') is one of the most popular dishes to emerge recently in Australia. It is a Hawaiian dish with a Japanese influence that uses seaweed, avocado and raw fish as its base. We love to serve ours on this coconut tortilla, but if you want a super-low-carb version, then serve it on cauliflower and broccoli rice (page 200) or some salad greens.

To make the poke dressing, combine all the ingredients in a bowl with 1 tablespoon of water, mix well and refrigerate for at least 30 minutes to allow the flavours to develop.

To make the coconut tortilla, combine the almond meal, tapioca flour, coconut milk, egg and 125 ml (½ cup) of water in a bowl, mix well and season with salt. Heat a small non-stick frying pan over medium heat. Add enough oil to coat the surface of the pan, then pour in 3 tablespoons of batter and swirl around slightly. Cook for 2 ½ minutes until mostly cooked through, then flip and cook for 3 minutes until golden and crisp. Place the tortilla on a plate and keep warm. Repeat with the remaining mixture to make six tortillas (see Tip below).

Slightly crush the avocado with a fork or potato masher and mix in the lime juice and olive oil. Season with salt and pepper.

Heat the coconut oil or fat in a frying pan over medium heat. Crack in the eggs and cook for 2–3 minutes, or until cooked to your liking. Season with salt and pepper. Keep warm.

Place the cucumber in a bowl, pour over 1 tablespoon of poke dressing and toss to combine. Set aside.

Add the tuna to the remaining poke dressing and gently toss. Taste and season with a little salt, if needed.

To serve, place a tortilla on each serving plate. Spoon on the avocado mixture, then top with the dressed cucumber and tuna. Squeeze a little lime juice over the tuna as desired, then add a fried egg. Sprinkle on some sesame seeds and serve with the coriander leaves.

TIP

Reserve the remaining tortillas for another use. They can be stored in an airtight container in the fridge for up to 1 week or frozen for up to 3 months.

PICKLED BEETROOT EGGS WITH SMOKED SALMON AND AVOCADO SALAD

SERVES 4

1 large beetroot, peeled and grated
170 ml (⅔ cup) apple cider vinegar
1 teaspoon sea salt
1 teaspoon black peppercorns
2 bay leaves
8 eggs, at room temperature

SALAD

200 g thinly sliced smoked salmon
1 large handful of salad leaves
2 avocados, cut into
    bite-sized pieces
80 ml (⅓ cup) extra-virgin olive oil
2 tablespoons apple cider vinegar
sea salt and freshly ground
    black pepper
2 tablespoons salmon roe
1 small handful of dill fronds
finely grated fresh horseradish,
    to serve (optional)

Whenever I have excess eggs, I love to flavour them – as I have here with beetroot – or ferment them to make a probiotic powerhouse of good fats and protein. Making beetroot eggs is super simple. For a complete meal the whole family will enjoy, simply team them with gorgeous salad ingredients and your protein of choice: in this case I have used salmon, as the combination of eggs, fish and salad works a treat.

You will need a wide-mouth 1 litre glass preserving jar for this recipe. To sterilise the jar, wash it in very hot, soapy water and run it through a hot rinse cycle in your dishwasher. If you don't have a dishwasher, boil the jar in a large saucepan of boiling water for 10 minutes, then transfer to a baking tray and place in a 150°C oven for 10 minutes, or until completely dry.

Place the beetroot and 500 ml of water in a saucepan and bring to the boil. Reduce the heat and simmer for 2 minutes until the beetroot is tender. Strain, reserving the liquid and cooked beetroot, and allow to cool. Place the beetroot in a container, cover and transfer to the fridge until needed.

To make the pickling brine, combine the beetroot liquid, vinegar, salt, peppercorns and bay leaves in a glass bowl or jug and stir well. Set aside.

Place the eggs in a saucepan of rapidly simmering water and cook for 5 minutes (for soft-boiled), or until cooked to your liking. Remove with a slotted spoon and peel when cool enough to handle.

Carefully place the eggs in the sterilised jar and pour over the pickling brine, making sure the eggs are fully submerged. If you need more liquid, add a little more water and vinegar. Cover with the lid and place in the fridge for at least 8 hours and up to 2 days.

When the eggs are ready, prepare the salad. Arrange the smoked salmon, salad leaves, avocado and grated beetroot on serving plates. Drizzle the olive oil and vinegar over the salad leaves and avocado and season with salt and pepper. Cut the pickled eggs in half, then add to the salad. Spoon the salmon roe over the top, scatter on the dill and grated horseradish (if using) and serve.

PAN-FRIED SALMON WITH THAI CUCUMBER SALAD

SERVES 4

2 tablespoons coconut oil or
 good-quality animal fat*, melted
4 × 160 g salmon fillets, skin on
sea salt

DRESSING
2 garlic cloves, finely chopped
3 tablespoons lime juice
1 tablespoon fish sauce
½ teaspoon ground coriander
½ teaspoon coconut sugar
1 tablespoon extra-virgin olive oil

THAI CUCUMBER SALAD
3–4 Lebanese cucumbers,
 cut into 1.5 cm dice
⅓ red onion, finely diced
1 large handful of mint leaves, torn
1 large handful of coriander leaves

TO SERVE
Sauerkraut (page 295)
micro herbs
lime wedges

* See Glossary

You may have noticed a theme running through this book that has little to do with low carb, healthy fat. I'm referring to the notion that you can have just a few ingredients on your plate and that is all you need for a beautiful, nutritious meal. And that is exactly what we have here with this delicious recipe: a simple salad teamed with a pan-fried piece of fatty fish.

Preheat the oven to 200°C.

To make the dressing, combine all the ingredients in a small bowl and mix well. Set aside.

To make the salad, place the cucumber, onion, mint and coriander in a bowl, add the dressing and gently toss to coat. Set aside.

Heat the oil or fat in a large non-stick ovenproof frying pan over medium–high heat. Season the salmon on both sides with salt. Add the fish, skin-side down, to the pan and cook for 2 minutes. Transfer the pan to the oven and roast the salmon for 2–3 minutes until the skin is golden and crisp. Remove the pan from the oven, flip the salmon over and set aside to cook for 30 seconds, or until medium–rare. (The residual heat from the pan will cook the salmon, so the pan doesn't need to be placed over heat.)

Place the salmon on serving plates, add the cucumber salad and some sauerkraut, scatter on the micro herbs and serve with the lime wedges.

ROASTED SPICED SALMON WITH GRILLED COS AND GREEN GODDESS DRESSING

SERVES 4

4 × 170 g salmon fillets, pin-boned
   and skin removed (if you like,
   you can keep the skin on)
½ teaspoon dried oregano
½ teaspoon dried mint
1 tablespoon finely chopped
   preserved lemon zest
   (inner flesh discarded)
coconut oil or good-quality animal
   fat*, melted, for brushing
sea salt and freshly ground
   black pepper
2 lemons, halved
4 baby cos lettuces, quartered
   lengthways
200 ml Green Goddess Dressing
   (page 288)

BAHARAT SPICE MIX

1 ½ tablespoons freshly ground
   black pepper
1 tablespoon ground coriander
1 tablespoon ground cinnamon
1 tablespoon ground cloves
1 ½ tablespoons ground cumin
½ teaspoon ground cardamom
1 tablespoon ground nutmeg
1 teaspoon ground ginger
2 tablespoons paprika

* See Glossary

Baharat, the Arabic word for 'spice', is a combination of Middle Eastern spices that work particularly well together. Fabulous for flavouring fish, meat, eggs, vegetables, mayo and fermented vegetables, it is available from good spice shops or online retailers, or why not try making your own? Here, I have teamed it with some lovely fatty salmon and grilled lettuce. If you aren't too keen on the grilled lettuce, simply keep it raw and this dish will still taste amazing.

To make the baharat spice mix, combine all ingredients in a bowl and mix well. Store leftover spice mix in an airtight container or jar in the pantry.

Rub the salmon fillets with the baharat spice mix, dried oregano, dried mint and preserved lemon until well coated. Cover and marinate for 1 hour in the fridge.

Preheat the oven to 200°C.

Brush the salmon fillets with some melted oil or fat and season with salt and pepper.

Heat an ovenproof non-stick frying pan over medium–high heat. Add the salmon fillets and cook for 30 seconds until lightly golden, then flip over and cook for another 30 seconds, or until golden. Transfer to the oven and cook for 4 minutes (for medium–rare), or until cooked to your liking.

Meanwhile, heat a chargrill pan or frying pan over medium–high heat. Brush the pan with some oil or fat, add the lemon halves, cut-side down, and cook for 2 minutes until caramelised. Remove from the pan and set aside, keeping warm.

Brush a little more oil on the pan, add the cos lettuce quarters and cook for 2 minutes on each side until slightly wilted and charred. Season with salt and pepper.

To serve, place the salmon on serving plates and arrange the grilled cos and lemon alongside. Drizzle the green goddess dressing over the cos and serve.

TOGARASHI SNAPPER WITH SAUTÉED GREENS AND CURRY MAYONNAISE

SERVES 2

250 g broccoli, broken into florets
2 × 170 g snapper fillets, skin on
2 tablespoons coconut oil or
    good-quality animal fat*, melted
sea salt and freshly ground
    black pepper
3 garlic cloves, finely chopped
1 long red chilli, deseeded and
    finely chopped
¼ bunch of kale (about 150 g),
    stems discarded and leaves torn
1 tablespoon apple cider vinegar
80 ml (⅓ cup) Fish or Chicken Bone
    Broth (pages 287 and 284)
    or water
1 teaspoon shichimi togarashi*
2 tablespoons extra-virgin olive oil

CURRY MAYONNAISE
80 g Mayonnaise (page 292)
1 teaspoon curry powder

* See Glossary

Togarashi, a Japanese spice mix of sesame seeds, chilli, citrus, pepper, garlic and seaweed, is super simple to make and turns the humblest of dishes into something extraordinary. If you are like me, you will be reaching for it daily to add a little love to your meals. Togarashi can make a slice of cucumber or avocado or some mayo dance on your palate, so go ahead and give it a go – but be warned: it can be very addictive.

Blanch the broccoli in boiling salted water for about 3 minutes until tender. Immediately plunge into ice-cold water to stop the cooking process. When the broccoli is completely cold, drain and set aside.

To make the curry mayonnaise, mix the ingredients in a small bowl to combine.

Brush the fish with a little coconut oil or fat and season with salt and pepper. Heat a frying pan over medium heat. Add the snapper, skin-side down, and cook for 3–3 ½ minutes. Turn and cook for 1 minute. Transfer to a plate.

Wipe the pan clean, return the pan to medium heat and add the remaining coconut oil or fat. Add the garlic and chilli and sauté for 30 seconds until fragrant. Add the kale and broccoli and sauté for 2 minutes until the kale is wilted. Season with salt and pepper.

Move the vegetables to one side and return the snapper, skin-side up, to the pan. Pour in the vinegar and broth or water, sprinkle the togarashi over the fish and cook for 1–2 minutes until the fish is cooked through. Drizzle over the olive oil and serve with the curry mayonnaise.

TIP
You can also use barramundi, ling, Spanish mackerel, john dory, bream or your favourite fish.

BANH MI LETTUCE WRAPS

SERVES 4

1 tablespoon tamari or
  coconut aminos*
1 tablespoon extra-virgin olive oil
  or macadamia oil
1–2 heads of baby cos lettuce,
  trimmed and leaves separated
80 g Chicken Liver Pâté (page 56)
400 g leftover roast chicken, sliced
1 large handful of mixed herbs
  (such as coriander, Vietnamese
  mint, mint, Thai basil)
2 long red chillies, deseeded
  and cut into matchsticks
1 spring onion, green part cut into
  long, thin strips
10 macadamia nuts (activated if
  possible*), toasted and chopped
100 g Kimchi (page 290), to serve
lime cheeks, to serve

PICKLED CARROT AND DAIKON
250 ml (1 cup) apple cider vinegar
1 small carrot, cut into matchsticks
¼ daikon, cut into matchsticks

* See Glossary

Vietnamese cuisine has been all the rage in Australia for the past decade or so, and rightly so, as it mixes the best South-East Asian ingredients with French culinary traditions. And this is shown in their very famous dish banh mi (which means bread wheat). I have taken a little creative licence here and turned this much-loved classic into a low-carb, healthy version that still retains the essence of the dish: pâté, roasted or grilled meat, cucumber, coriander and carrot or onion. These banh mi lettuce wraps are a great way to introduce liver into your family's diet and will become a firm favourite.

To make the pickled carrot and daikon, combine the vinegar and 100 ml of warm water in a saucepan over medium heat. Transfer to a bowl or container and set aside. When cool, add the carrot and daikon, cover and refrigerate for at least 2 hours or, for best results, overnight.

Mix the tamari or coconut aminos with 1 tablespoon of water and the olive or macadamia oil. Set aside.

Arrange the lettuce leaves on a platter and top with the pâté, then layer on the chicken, pickled carrot and daikon, mixed herbs, chilli and spring onion. Drizzle on the tamari or coconut aminos dressing, sprinkle over the chopped macadamias and serve with the kimchi and lime cheeks on the side.

TIP
If you like it spicy, add a thinly sliced bird's eye chilli or a pinch of chilli flakes to 2 teaspoons of tamari or coconut aminos and drizzle over the lettuce wraps.

CHICKEN WINGS WITH TOMATO, BASIL AND GREENS

SERVES 4–6

3 tablespoons coconut oil

1.5 kg chicken wings, cut into wingettes and drummettes

2 onions, chopped

4 garlic cloves, crushed

250 ml (1 cup) white wine

600 g canned whole peeled tomatoes

2 bay leaves

2 teaspoons finely chopped rosemary leaves

80 g pitted black olives (optional)

2 tablespoons chopped flat-leaf parsley leaves

125 ml (½ cup) Chicken Bone Broth (page 284)

sea salt and freshly ground black pepper

2 silverbeet leaves, stems removed and leaves roughly chopped

1 tablespoon apple cider vinegar

basil sprigs, to serve

3 tablespoons extra-virgin olive oil

This is a bit of a go-to dish at home, as we always have organic chicken wings in the freezer – not only because they are delicious but also because they are budget-friendly and we love eating with our hands. You can pretty much use any protein with this sauce, such as meatballs from grass-fed cattle, lamb shanks or seafood, and if wings are not your cup of tea then some chicken legs will work a treat as well.

Preheat the oven to 180°C.

Heat the coconut oil in a large, deep ovenproof frying pan or casserole dish over medium–high heat. Cook the chicken wings, in batches, for 3 minutes on each side, or until golden. Remove from the pan and set aside.

Reduce the heat to medium, add the onion to the pan and cook for 8 minutes, or until translucent. Add the garlic and cook for a further 1 minute. Add the wine and cook for about 5 minutes until it evaporates, then add the tomatoes (crushing with a wooden spoon), bay leaf, rosemary, olives (if using), parsley, chicken broth and chicken wings. Season to taste with salt and pepper.

Place the pan in the oven and cook for 35 minutes, then add the silverbeet leaves and gently mix through the sauce. Cook for a further 5 minutes, or until the chicken is cooked through.

Mix the apple cider vinegar through the sauce and serve scattered with the basil sprigs and drizzled with the olive oil.

MUSHROOM CHICKEN BURGER

SERVES 4

2 chicken breast fillets or
   4 chicken thigh fillets
80 ml (⅓ cup) coconut oil or
   good-quality animal fat*, melted
1 teaspoon finely grated lemon zest
sea salt and freshly ground
   black pepper
8 large portobello mushrooms
4 rindless bacon rashers
100 g (⅓ cup) Aioli (page 280)
1 avocado, sliced
4 cos lettuce leaves, torn

* See Glossary

Organic vegetables, good-quality fats and moderate amounts of protein from healthy animals is the simple formula for any meal you plan to eat. Follow this and meal times, shopping and cooking will become a breeze. Take, for instance, this recipe. We use great vegetables (mushrooms, lettuce, avocado – technically a fruit but full of healthy fats), add animal protein (chicken and fatty bacon) and fat (homemade aioli), and we have a breakfast, lunch or dinner for the whole family that can be whipped up in under 15 minutes. If the kids aren't keen on mushrooms, use the lettuce leaves as wraps or try paleo bread or cauliflower and bacon toast (page 118) as an alternative.

Preheat the oven to 220°C. Line a baking tray with baking paper.

Place the chicken between two sheets of baking paper and flatten with a mallet until 1 cm thick, then cut in half. Brush the chicken with 1 tablespoon of oil or fat, sprinkle over the lemon zest and season with salt and pepper. Set aside.

Remove the mushroom stems and place the mushroom caps, stem-side down, on the prepared tray. Drizzle with 1 tablespoon of oil or fat, season with salt and pepper and bake for 10 minutes until the mushrooms are tender. Place the mushrooms on paper towel to remove excess moisture and allow to cool.

Heat a barbecue hotplate to medium–hot. Add the remaining oil or fat and the chicken patties and bacon and cook for 2–2 ½ minutes. Turn the patties and bacon and continue to cook for a few minutes until the patties are cooked through and the bacon is crisp. Season with salt and pepper.

Place four mushroom caps, stem-side up, on serving plates or a platter. Smear a spoonful of aioli on each mushroom base, then layer on the avocado, chicken, bacon and cos leaves. Place a mushroom cap, stem-side down, on top and serve.

ITALIAN LIVER SPAGHETTI

SERVES 4–6

600 g zucchini (about 4)

2 tablespoons good-quality
  animal fat*

1 large onion, chopped

4 garlic cloves, finely chopped

2 tablespoons tomato paste

250 g field mushrooms (about 3),
  chopped

500 g chicken livers, trimmed
  and chopped into small dice

1 tablespoon chopped oregano
  leaves

80 ml (⅓ cup) red wine
  (such as shiraz)

2 × 400 g cans whole peeled
  tomatoes, crushed

250 ml (1 cup) Chicken Bone Broth
  (page 284), plus extra if needed

sea salt and freshly ground
  black pepper

pinch of chilli flakes (optional)

1 handful of basil leaves, shredded
  (optional)

2 macadamia nuts (activated if
  possible*), finely grated

2 tablespoons extra-virgin olive oil

* See Glossary

Of all the ingredients we should be eating for optimal health, you cannot beat liver in all its wonder. From a nutritional perspective, nothing comes close. It contains vitamins A, K2 and B12, calcium, magnesium and the list goes on and on. It is also delicious and cheap as chips. This recipe is a wonderful and creative way to get more liver into your diet. Play around with the ratios: start by using, say, 5 per cent liver to 95 per cent minced meat and then up the liver when the family gets used to and enjoys the taste.

To make the zucchini spaghetti, use the thick noodle blade on a spiraliser. If you don't have a spiraliser, use a sharp knife to cut the zucchini lengthways into long thin strips. Set aside until needed.

Melt the fat in a large frying pan over medium–high heat. Add the onion and cook for 5 minutes until softened. Stir in the garlic and cook for 30 seconds until fragrant and starting to brown. Add the tomato paste and cook for 1 minute, then stir in the mushrooms and cook for 4–5 minutes until softened. Add the liver and sauté for 1 minute, then add the oregano, pour in the wine and bring to the boil. Simmer for 2 minutes until the liquid has reduced by half. Stir in the crushed tomatoes and broth, reduce the heat to medium–low and simmer for 15 minutes until thickened and rich in flavour, adding more broth if needed. Season with salt and pepper.

Remove the sauce from the heat and stir in the zucchini spaghetti. Sprinkle the chilli flakes (if using), basil (if using) and grated macadamia over the top and serve with a drizzle of olive oil.

CHICKEN BASQUE WITH OLIVES AND ARTICHOKES

SERVES 5

2 teaspoons sea salt, plus extra
    to serve
1 teaspoon freshly ground
    black pepper, plus extra to serve
1 teaspoon smoked paprika
80 g tapioca flour
6 chicken thigh cutlets, bone in,
    skin on
80 ml (⅓ cup) good-quality
    animal fat*
2 onions, chopped
1 red capsicum, deseeded and sliced
4 garlic cloves, chopped
60 ml (¼ cup) apple cider vinegar
70 g kalamata olives, pitted
70 g manzanilla olives
    (or any green olives of your choice)
4 roma tomatoes, deseeded
    and chopped
200 g artichoke hearts, drained,
    rinsed and quartered
500 ml (2 cups) Chicken Bone
    Broth (page 284)
1 large handful of baby spinach leaves
zest and juice of ¼ lemon
1 small handful of basil leaves,
    to serve

* See Glossary

Braised chicken legs would have to be one of the all-time favourite dishes across the Mediterranean, as every country, if not every region, seems to have its own unique and delicious way of doing it. The key for me is to make sure you get chicken thighs, drumsticks, wings or whole marylands that still have the skin on, as you really want that mouth-watering tasty skin to give extra flavour and texture to the dish. Of course, it will work fine without it, but the chef in me – and also the health coach – suggests you keep the skin on for taste and health reasons. It is always best to source organic free-range chicken if you can, too. Here is a lovely Spanish-inspired dish to have up your sleeve for when you want to impress.

Combine the salt, pepper, smoked paprika and tapioca flour in a bowl. Add the chicken and coat evenly in the seasoned flour, shaking off any excess.

Preheat the oven 170°C.

Heat the fat in a large, deep ovenproof frying pan over medium–high heat. Cook the chicken, in batches, for 4 minutes skin-side down, then 2 minutes on the other side. Remove the chicken from the pan and set aside on a plate.

Reduce the heat to medium, add the onion and capsicum and cook for 5 minutes, or until softened. Add the garlic and cook for 30 seconds, then add the apple cider vinegar. Add the olives, tomato, artichoke and broth, then return the chicken to the pan and bring to the boil. Place in the oven to cook for 45 minutes, or until the chicken is tender.

To finish, gently mix through the spinach and season with salt and pepper. Sprinkle over the lemon zest, squeeze over the lemon juice and garnish with the basil leaves.

CHICKEN MARYLANDS WITH SALMORIGLIO

SERVES 5

5 chicken marylands
2 tablespoons coconut oil or
good-quality animal fat*,
plus extra for greasing
sea salt and freshly ground
black pepper
2 onions, cut crossways into
thick slices
1 garlic bulb, cloves separated
2 lemons, halved crossways
1 tablespoon finely chopped
rosemary leaves

SALMORIGLIO

3 garlic cloves
sea salt
2 bunches of oregano, leaves picked
1 bunch of flat-leaf parsley,
leaves picked
100 ml extra-virgin olive oil
juice of 1 lemon

* See Glossary

I want to introduce you to one of the easiest and tastiest sauces/marinades/dressings in the world: the southern Italian salmoriglio. Salmoriglio contains lemon juice, extra-virgin olive oil, garlic, salt and, of course, herbs – generally oregano and parsley. Fresh oregano is preferable, but if you can't find it then dried oregano is also fine. A little mint can sometimes be added, as well as some crushed fresh tomato if you like. I will leave it to you to decide how you want to make it, but I have included my very simple recipe below and teamed it with roasted chicken legs (with the skin on, of course). This sauce is also amazing on eggs, vegetables, fish, lamb and steak, so go to town on it!

To make the salmoriglio, pound the garlic with a pinch of salt to a paste using a mortar and pestle (or you can use a hand-held blender or food processor). Add the oregano and parsley, pound to a paste, then stir in the olive oil and lemon juice. Season to taste with salt.

Coat the chicken with the oil or fat and season with salt and pepper.

Preheat the oven to 200°C. Grease a roasting pan with some oil or fat, then scatter in the onion, garlic and lemon. Arrange the chicken on top and sprinkle with the rosemary.

Roast the chicken for 45–50 minutes, basting occasionally with the pan juices, until the chicken is cooked through and golden. Remove from the oven, spoon over the salmoriglio and serve.

AVOCADO BUN BURGER

SERVES 4

1 large beetroot
2 tablespoons coconut oil or
    good-quality animal fat*
1 onion, sliced into thin rings
4 rindless bacon rashers (optional)
4 avocados
2 gherkins, sliced, plus extra
    to serve
4 slices of tomato
2 butter lettuce leaves, torn into
    4 pieces
1 teaspoon black sesame seeds

PATTIES

350 g full-fat beef mince
¼ onion, finely diced
2 garlic cloves, crushed
1 egg
pinch of chilli flakes (optional)
1 tablespoon chopped flat-leaf
    parsley leaves
1 large pinch of dried oregano
1½ teaspoons sea salt
1 teaspoon freshly ground
    black pepper

CHIPOTLE MAYONNAISE

100 g (⅓ cup) Mayonnaise
    (page 292)
1 teaspoon chipotle powder
    or chilli powder

* See Glossary

How much fun is this little pocket rocket of a burger, which I have dubbed 'the fat deluxe'? A lot of the latest research tells us to eat more top-quality dietary fat. And you won't find a more delicious way to do that than with this dish. Creamy avocado, a melt-in-the-mouth burger patty and whatever other additions you love make this burger something to be enjoyed. Serve with some fermented veg on the side to make it a powerhouse of goodness.

Fill a saucepan with water and place a fitted steamer with a lid on top. Bring to the boil, place the beetroot in the steamer, cover and steam for 45 minutes until cooked through. To tell if the beetroot is cooked, insert a knife in the centre; if it slides in easily, it's ready. Plunge the beetroot into ice-cold water, then remove the skin with a damp cloth. (Remember to wear gloves!) Thinly slice the beetroot, transfer to a plate and set aside.

To make the patties, combine all the ingredients in a large bowl and mix well. Shape into four patties.

Heat a barbecue plate to medium–hot or a large chargrill pan over medium–high heat. Brush with the oil or fat, add the onion and cook, stirring occasionally, for 5 minutes. Add the patties and bacon (if using) and cook for 2 minutes. Turn the patties and bacon and cook for 2 minutes until the patties are cooked through, the bacon is crisp and the onion is caramelised. Remove from the heat and keep warm.

To make the chipotle mayonnaise, mix the mayonnaise and chilli powder together and season with a pinch of salt, if needed. Set aside.

To make the avocado bun, slice each avocado in half crossways. Remove the stone and peel away the skin. On the more rounded half of each avocado, slice off a small piece to form a flat base. (This helps the burger to stand on the plate.)

To assemble the burgers, place each avocado base, cavity-side up, on a serving plate. Spread 1 teaspoon of chipotle mayonnaise on each avocado base. Top with a patty, the sliced gherkin, onion, bacon (if using), tomato, lettuce and beetroot. Spread on another teaspoon of chipotle mayonnaise, then add the top half of the avocado bun. Sprinkle on the sesame seeds and serve with the extra gherkins on the side.

PORK SAN CHOY BAU WITH FRIED EGG

SERVES 4

3 tablespoons coconut oil or
  good-quality animal fat*
4 garlic cloves, finely chopped
4 red Asian shallots, chopped
2 teaspoons finely grated ginger
600 g pork mince
100 g shiitake mushrooms, chopped
2 ½ tablespoons tamari or
  coconut aminos*
1 tablespoon fish sauce,
  plus extra to serve
125 ml (½ cup) Chicken or Beef
  Bone Broth (pages 284 and 282)
1 × 225 g can water chestnuts,
  drained and finely chopped
2 spring onions, white and green
  parts, thinly sliced
1–2 long red chillies, deseeded
  and chopped, plus 1 extra long red
  or bird's eye chilli, sliced, to serve
8 eggs
sea salt and freshly ground
  black pepper
8 iceberg lettuce leaves
80 g bean sprouts

TO SERVE

1 spring onion, green part only,
  thinly sliced
coriander leaves, torn
toasted sesame seeds
Sauerkraut (page 295)
  or Kimchi (page 290)

* See Glossary

One of my all-time favourite Chinese dishes is the very moreish san choy bau, a mixture of meat, veg, spices and herbs wrapped in a lettuce or cabbage leaf. Regarding the type of meat to use, the easiest is mince of any kind – try pork, beef, lamb, chicken, duck, quail, kangaroo, venison or a mix of any of these – and the fattier the better, or you can use seafood like crabmeat, diced prawns or fish. If you can pop in some offal, such as liver, heart, sweetbreads, brains, marrow or kidney, that is a bonus. I have taken the liberty of adding a fried egg, but you can leave it out or make a simple thin omelette and slice it to go on top.

Heat a wok or large frying pan over medium–high heat.
Add 1 tablespoon of oil or fat and swirl around the wok or pan.
Add the garlic, shallot and ginger and cook for 1 minute. Add the pork and mushrooms and cook, stirring occasionally, for a further 4–5 minutes until the pork is browned and cooked through. Add the tamari or coconut aminos and fish sauce and toss to mix. Next, pour in the broth and cook until reduced by half. Stir in the water chestnuts, spring onion and chilli and cook for 1–2 minutes until heated through and the liquid has almost gone. Remove from the heat and check for seasoning, adding more fish sauce if needed.

Meanwhile, heat the remaining oil or fat in a large non-stick frying pan over medium heat. Crack the eggs into the pan, in batches, and cook for 2–3 minutes, or until cooked to your liking. Season the eggs with salt and pepper, slide onto a plate and keep warm.

Place the lettuce cups on a large serving platter or on plates. Top each with some pork mixture and an egg, then scatter on the bean sprouts and extra chilli. Serve with the spring onion, coriander leaves, sesame seeds and sauerkraut or kimchi on the side.

PORK BELLY TERRINE

SERVES 8

2 tablespoons coconut oil or
good-quality animal fat*,
plus extra for greasing
1 onion, finely chopped
1 teaspoon chopped rosemary
leaves
1 teaspoon chopped thyme leaves
4 garlic cloves, finely chopped
100 ml white wine (such as
chardonnay)
400 g boned pork belly, rind
removed, cut into 5 cm dice
140 g pork back fat, cut into
5 mm dice (see Note)
220 g chicken livers, trimmed
and cut into 5 mm dice
500 g pork mince
3 tablespoons chopped
curly parsley
1 tablespoon sea salt
2 teaspoons freshly ground
black pepper
2 egg yolks

TO SERVE
thyme sprigs
pickled vegetables
caperberries
Sauerkraut (page 295)

* See Glossary

If there is one recipe in this book I encourage you to make, it is this terrine, which is basically a fancy meatloaf. Once you try it, I believe you will become addicted not only to the flavour but also to the simple process, as you can make so much with so little effort. The options of what you can include are almost endless. Some of the favourites I like to play around with are other types of minced meat, such as duck, chicken and rabbit, different nuts, seeds, herbs and spices and offal, such as sweetbreads and liver.

Heat the oil or fat in a frying pan over medium–low heat. Add the onion and sauté for 10 minutes until softened and translucent. Add the rosemary, thyme, garlic and white wine, bring to the boil and cook until the liquid has reduced to 2 tablespoons. Remove from the heat and allow to cool.

Place the pork belly in a large bowl, add the pork back fat, chicken livers, pork mince, cooled onion mixture, parsley, salt and pepper and mix well. Cover and place in the fridge for 1 hour.

Preheat the oven to 140°C. Grease a 20 cm × 10 cm loaf tin and line the base and sides with baking paper, allowing enough overhang on the long sides to enclose the top of the terrine.

Remove the pork belly mixture from the fridge, add the egg yolks and mix well. Pack the mixture firmly into the prepared tin, ensuring there are no air bubbles. Fold the overhanging paper over the terrine to cover and smooth the top with your hands. Wrap the whole terrine tightly with a double layer of foil and place in a large baking dish. Pour in enough boiling water to reach halfway up the sides of the tin. Bake for 2 hours until a thermometer inserted in the centre of the terrine reaches 72°C. Remove the terrine from the baking dish and, still covered in foil, set aside to cool to room temperature.

For best results and easy slicing, press your terrine as it cools. Find a piece of plastic or wood that fits snugly on top of the terrine tin and weigh it down with a brick or two, or you can use another similar-sized loaf tin with a brick inside. Transfer to the fridge to set overnight.

Remove the terrine from the tin. (Dipping the tin into a warm water bath can help.) Remove the baking paper and clean any jelly or fat residue on the terrine with paper towel. Cut the terrine into 1 cm thick slices, scatter over the thyme sprigs, sprinkle on some salt and pepper and serve with the pickled vegetables, caperberries and sauerkraut.

NOTE
You can buy pork back fat
from your local butcher.
It may need to be ordered
in advance.

PORK SAUSAGES WITH KRAUT AND MUSTARD

SERVES 4

2 tablespoons coconut oil or
   good-quality animal fat*
8 paleo pork sausages
   (see Note)
100 ml Jus (page 289)
seeded mustard, to serve
200 g Sauerkraut (page 295),
   to serve
dill fronds, to serve

* See Glossary

If you travel through Germany and Austria, you'll notice traditional farmhouses where you can get a meal. Some of these farmhouses only serve food they grow themselves. So, what can you expect? Well, basically, they serve paleo and low-carb broths and soups and dishes made from pork sausages, cured meats and offal that are accompanied by leafy greens and fermented vegetables. All of this can be washed down with a good-quality apple cider or other fermented drink. This simple recipe of snags, mustard and kraut is in honour of those wonderful farmhouses.

Heat the oil or fat in a large frying pan over medium heat. Add the sausages and cook until browned on all sides and just cooked through (about 8 minutes). Remove from the heat.

Meanwhile, heat the jus in a small saucepan over medium–low heat.

To serve, spoon some mustard onto serving plates, add the sauerkraut and sausages, then drizzle on the jus and scatter over the dill.

NOTE
Paleo sausages are grain free and derived from grass-fed animals.

CHORIZO MINCE WITH FRIED EGGS AND LEAFY GREENS

SERVES 4

3 tablespoons coconut oil or
   good-quality animal fat*
1 onion, finely chopped
1 red capsicum, chopped into
   small dice
4 garlic cloves, finely chopped
500 g pork mince
1 ½ teaspoons ground cumin
1 teaspoon ground coriander
1 teaspoon smoked paprika
1 teaspoon sweet paprika
1 teaspoon chilli flakes
1 teaspoon dried oregano
2 tablespoons apple cider vinegar
2 tablespoons tomato paste
500 ml (2 cups) Beef or Chicken
   Bone Broth (pages 282 and 284)
   or water
sea salt and freshly ground
   black pepper
4 eggs
1 handful of watercress
1 small handful of baby salad leaves
1 tablespoon extra-virgin olive oil
1 ½ teaspoons lime juice or apple
   cider vinegar
Chilli Oil (page 285), to serve
   (optional)

* See Glossary

If you have any of my other books, you will have noticed that I love to team mince with eggs – and there are a few very good reasons for this. First, the combination is one of the cheapest, most readily available sources of good fats and protein: both ingredients can be bought in every supermarket. Second, it is simple to make. Third, it is bloody delicious. Fourth, you can eat this for breakfast, lunch or dinner, as it ticks all the boxes. Finally, you can make up heaps of cooked mince and freeze it in portions so you always have some on hand to thaw, then you just need to fry or poach an egg and add some greens, vegetables or salad and your meal is ready.

Heat 2 tablespoons of oil or fat in a large frying pan over medium heat. Add the onion and capsicum and cook for 5–8 minutes until softened. Stir in the garlic and cook for 30 seconds until softened.

Increase the heat to medium–high, add the pork to the pan and cook, stirring with a wooden spoon to break up any lumps, for 5–6 minutes until lightly browned. Add all the spices, the oregano, vinegar and tomato paste, cook for 30 seconds, then pour in the broth or water. Stir well and bring to the boil. Reduce the heat to low and simmer gently for 10–15 minutes until the liquid is reduced by half. You still want the mince to be slightly saucy and juicy. If the liquid has reduced too much and the mince is dry, stir through a little more broth or water to moisten. Season with salt and pepper.

Meanwhile, heat the remaining oil or fat in a non-stick frying pan over medium heat. Crack the eggs into the pan and cook for 2–3 minutes, or until cooked to your liking. Season the eggs with salt and pepper and slide onto a plate. Keep warm.

Place the watercress and salad leaves in a bowl and gently toss with the olive oil and lime juice or vinegar until the leaves are lightly dressed. Season with salt and pepper.

Divide the chorizo mince between serving plates, then top with a fried egg, some salad leaves and a drizzle of chilli oil, if you wish.

ROAST PORK BELLY SALAD WITH SESAME DRESSING

SERVES 4–6

900 g boned pork belly
1 tablespoon lard or other
  good-quality animal fat*
sea salt
1 tablespoon shichimi togarashi*,
  or to taste

SESAME DRESSING

2 tablespoons hulled tahini
2 tablespoons tamari or
  coconut aminos*
2 tablespoons apple cider vinegar
1 tablespoon honey (optional)
2 garlic cloves, finely chopped
1 tablespoon finely grated ginger
2 tablespoons sesame oil
2 tablespoons extra-virgin olive oil

SALAD

¼ Chinese cabbage (wong bok)
  (about 280 g), shredded
4 spring onions, cut into thin strips
1 large carrot, cut into matchsticks
1 cucumber, deseeded and
  cut into matchsticks
1 large handful of alfalfa sprouts
  (about 80 g)
1 large handful of mixed salad leaves
1 large handful of coriander leaves
80 g (½ cup) pine nuts, toasted
1 ½ tablespoons toasted
  sesame seeds

* See Glossary

Whenever we roast pork belly, I always make extra so that we can enjoy some the next day with a salad for breakfast, lunch or dinner. Once you have that gorgeous meat in the fridge, all you need do is combine it with whatever you have on hand that inspires you. Team it with a dressing or sauce and, voila, you have a lovely low-carb, healthy-fat dish that really can't be beaten. If you are making the pork belly a day or two ahead, to keep the crackling crisp, remove it from the roast pork and let it cool down, then pop it into an airtight container and store it in the fridge.

Preheat the oven to 240°C (you need to start by blasting the pork with heat).

Place the pork belly on a wire rack in the kitchen sink, carefully pour boiling water over the pork skin and pat dry with paper towel.

Rub the pork skin with the lard or fat, season with salt and place in a large roasting tin. Roast for about 35–40 minutes until the skin starts to bubble. Reduce the temperature to 150°C and continue to roast the pork belly for 1 hour until tender. Remove from the oven and allow to rest. If the crackling doesn't crackle enough, place the pork belly, crackling-side up, under a hot grill for a few minutes. Sprinkle over the togarashi.

To make the sesame dressing, combine all the ingredients in a bowl and mix well.

To make the salad, combine all the ingredients in a large bowl and gently toss.

Cut the pork into thick slices and serve with the salad and sesame dressing.

BLAT WRAP

SERVES 4

8 rindless streaky bacon rashers
150 g Mayonnaise (page 292)
4 Nut-free Paleo Wraps (page 294)
¼ iceberg lettuce, shredded
    (about 100 g)
1 avocado, sliced
1 large tomato, sliced
sea salt and freshly ground
    black pepper

* See Glossary

Bacon, lettuce, avocado and tomato (BLAT) is a classic flavour combination generally associated with breakfast or brunch; however, I think it works well any time of day. Here, by replacing the high-carb element of the dish – the bread – with an egg-based wrap, I have added good-quality fats and protein to provide longer and more sustained energy, so you will not feel ravenous an hour or two later. Try this out on the family for a weekend breakfast or brunch and I guarantee it will become one of their favourites. Oh, and if you want to get a little fancy, wrap the whole thing in a nori sheet. Trust me on this one!

Preheat the oven to 200°C. Grease and line a large baking tray with baking paper.

Place the bacon in a single layer on the prepared tray, making sure the strips do not touch. Bake, turning the tray once for an even cook, for 12 minutes until the bacon is golden and crisp. Keep a close eye on the bacon to prevent it from burning.

Spread the mayonnaise on the paleo wraps, then divide the shredded lettuce, crispy bacon, avocado and tomato between them. Season with salt and pepper, roll up each wrap and serve.

PORK PATTIES WITH FRIED EGGS AND GREENS

SERVES 4

2 teaspoons cumin seeds
2 teaspoons coriander seeds
½ teaspoon freshly ground
white pepper
sea salt and freshly ground
black pepper
550 g pork mince
2 garlic cloves, finely chopped
1 teaspoon finely chopped
thyme leaves
1 ½ tablespoons chopped
flat-leaf parsley leaves
3 tablespoons coconut oil or
good-quality animal fat*
½ bunch of silverbeet (about 330 g),
stems removed and leaves torn
(save the stems for broths)
4 eggs
1 small handful of chives,
finely snipped
Chilli Oil (page 285), to serve

* See Glossary

I love the simplicity of a dish like this for the whole family: a fatty and delicious pork burger patty with a runny fried egg on top and some greens underneath to soak up the amazing meaty flavours and egg yolk 'sauce'. You can make this with any type of mince: turkey, lamb, duck, beef or pork, as we have here, and season and spice it however you see fit. Serve with a side of fermented veg and/or a base of cauliflower and bacon toast (page 118) or a grilled field or portobello mushroom and you are in burger bliss territory.

Heat a frying pan over medium heat, add the cumin and coriander seeds and toast for 1 minute until fragrant. Allow to cool.

Grind the toasted spices, white pepper and 1 teaspoon of salt to a fine powder using a spice grinder or mortar and pestle.

Place the pork, garlic, thyme, ground spices and parsley in a bowl and mix by hand to combine. Cover and refrigerate for 20 minutes to allow the flavours to infuse into the meat.

Divide the meat mixture into four portions and shape into patties about 8 cm in diameter and 2 cm thick.

Heat 1 tablespoon of oil or fat in a large non-stick frying pan over medium heat. Add the patties and cook for 4 minutes on each side until cooked through and golden. Keep warm.

Meanwhile, heat 1 tablespoon of oil or fat in another non-stick frying pan over medium heat. Add the silverbeet and sauté for 2 minutes until just wilted. Season with salt and pepper. Remove from the pan and set aside, keeping warm.

Wipe the pan clean, add the remaining oil or fat and heat over medium–low heat. Carefully crack the eggs into the pan and cook, undisturbed, for 2–3 minutes until the whites are cooked through and the yolks are still runny, or until cooked to your liking.

Divide the silverbeet among serving plates, then top each portion with a patty and fried egg. To finish, sprinkle over the snipped chives, drizzle with some chilli oil and season with a little salt and pepper.

SPICED PORK CHOPS WITH APPLE AND RHUBARB SALSA

SERVES 4

4 pork loin chops
    (about 220 g each)
3 tablespoons coconut oil or
    good-quality animal fat*, melted
1 large handful of dill fronds
1 large handful of coriander leaves

APPLE AND RHUBARB SALSA

5 rhubarb stalks, peeled and
    cut into 5 mm dice
1 green apple, peeled, cored
    and cut into small dice
1 spring onion, finely chopped
1 ½ tablespoons apple cider vinegar
2 tablespoons honey (optional)
80 ml (⅓ cup) extra-virgin olive oil,
    plus extra to serve
1 tablespoon chopped coriander
    leaves
sea salt

SPICE RUB

2 tablespoons fennel seeds
1 tablespoon whole aniseed
1 tablespoon ground piment
    d'Espelette (see Note)
1 teaspoon garlic powder
1 teaspoon freshly ground
    black pepper
2 teaspoons sea salt

* See Glossary

I remember as a kid Mum used to cook pork and lamb chops quite regularly – and I loved cutting through the fatty meaty parts to get at all that flavour and texture. I encourage you to go out and get some wonderful fatty pork or lamb chops and fire up the barbie or frying pan and bring the fat back to your dinner table. You can team your chops with any salad or veggies you like, but for something fancy try this rhubarb salsa.

To make the rhubarb salsa, blanch the rhubarb in boiling water for 10 seconds, then plunge into ice-cold water. Drain well, then mix with the remaining ingredients in a bowl. Set aside to allow the flavours to develop for 10 minutes.

Meanwhile, to make the spice rub, place the fennel seeds and aniseed in a spice grinder or mortar and grind to a powder. Transfer to a bowl and mix through the remaining spice ingredients.

Preheat the oven to 180°C.

Brush the pork chops with half the coconut oil or fat, then coat thoroughly with the spice rub.

Heat a large frying pan over high heat, add half the remaining coconut oil or fat and brown two pork chops for about 2 minutes on each side. Wipe out the pan and repeat with the remaining coconut oil or fat and pork chops. Transfer the chops to a baking tray and roast in the oven for 2 minutes, flip the chops over and return to the oven to roast for a further 2–3 minutes (for medium), or until cooked to your liking. Allow to rest for 3 minutes before cutting into 2 cm slices.

Place the pork on serving plates or a platter. Season with salt and serve with the rhubarb salsa, dill and coriander and a drizzle of olive oil.

NOTE

Piment d'Espelette is a type of chilli, with a warm fruity flavour and a mild chilli bite, that comes from the Basque region of France. It can be purchased from some delis, fine food stores or online. If you can't find it, hot paprika is a perfect substitute.

BLOOD SAUSAGE WITH FRIED EGG AND CHIMICHURRI

SERVES 2

1 bunch of broccolini (about 220 g), trimmed and halved

1 tablespoon coconut oil or good-quality animal fat*

200 g grain-free blood sausage, peeled and cut into 8 slices

2 eggs

CHIMICHURRI

3 garlic cloves, peeled

sea salt

1 long red chilli, deseeded and chopped

1 large handful of flat-leaf parsley leaves

1 large handful of coriander leaves

1 small handful of oregano leaves

80 ml (⅓ cup) apple cider vinegar

¼ teaspoon ground cumin

150 ml extra-virgin olive oil

freshly ground black pepper

* See Glossary

If I was to pick the meals I could eat on my last day on this planet in this body, then this would definitely be one of them. If you have never eaten blood sausage (or black pudding as it is sometimes called), I urge you to try it ASAP. Blood sausage is prepared in lots of different cultures around the globe and the base ingredients are the same: the blood, fat and meat of a pig mixed with spices. It is important to source blood sausage that is grain and dairy free, or have a go at making it yourself. Blood sausage is awesome with fried eggs or chopped up in a bolognese or shepherd's pie. I have teamed it here with some broccolini and a simple chimichurri sauce to make it shine.

To make the chimichurri, place the garlic and a small pinch of salt in a mortar and crush with the pestle. Add the chilli, parsley, coriander and oregano and pound to a paste. Stir in the vinegar, cumin and olive oil, then taste and season with salt and pepper. Alternatively, place all the ingredients in the bowl of a food processor and pulse a few times until the herbs are finely chopped and combined.

Blanch the broccolini in boiling salted water for 2–3 minutes until tender, then drain well. Set aside, keeping warm.

Heat 1 teaspoon of oil or fat in a frying pan over medium–high heat. Add the blood sausage slices and fry for 2 minutes on each side until cooked through and crisp. Keep a close eye on them, as the dark colour can make it hard to tell when they are done. Carefully remove the blood sausage slices from the pan and transfer to a plate, keeping warm.

Wipe the pan clean with paper towel, then add the remaining oil and heat over medium heat. Crack the eggs into the pan and cook for 2–3 minutes, or until cooked to your liking. Season with salt and pepper.

Slide the eggs onto serving plates, add the blood sausage and broccolini, then drizzle with some chimichurri and serve.

TIP

The remaining chimichurri can be refrigerated in an airtight container for up to 1 week. It's a perfect sauce for beef, fish and vegetable dishes.

PALEO HOT DOGS

SERVES 2–4

3 ½ tablespoons coconut oil or
   good-quality animal fat*
1 large onion, sliced
sea salt and freshly ground
   black pepper
2 rindless bacon rashers, chopped
4 paleo sausages (see Note
   page 167) (beef, pork or any
   of your choice)
4 baby cos lettuce leaves
50 g Sauerkraut (page 295)
3 tablespoons Tomato Ketchup
   (page 296)
3 tablespoons English or
   Dijon mustard

* See Glossary

Well, these little beauties are not the kind of hot dogs you would get in New York City, but they are a hell of a lot healthier and, I believe, tastier. You can use normal gluten-free sausages for this recipe or there are actually really good-quality hot dogs now available, made from meat with no added nasties. Either way, the whole family will love this low-carb version of a perennial favourite.

Melt 2 tablespoons of the oil or fat in a non-stick frying pan over medium heat. Add the onion and sauté for 8 minutes until translucent and starting to caramelise. Season with salt and pepper. Remove the onion from the pan and keep warm.

Wipe the pan clean with paper towel. Place the pan back over medium heat with ½ tablespoon of oil or fat. Add the bacon and cook for 6–8 minutes, stirring occasionally, until golden and slightly crispy. Set aside and keep warm.

Heat the remaining oil or fat in a non-stick frying over medium heat. Cook the sausages for about 8 minutes until cooked through and coloured all over.

Slice the sausages in half lengthways, without cutting all the way through. Place them lengthways in the centre of each lettuce leaf. Scatter over the onion, bacon and sauerkraut, then spoon over some ketchup and mustard and serve.

INDIAN-SPICED LAMB CHOPS WITH MINT CHUTNEY

SERVES 4

8 lamb chops
2 tablespoons coconut oil, melted
lemon wedges, to serve
toasted cumin seeds, to serve

CRISPY CURRY LEAVES

150 g coconut oil
4 sprigs of curry leaves
sea salt

MINT CHUTNEY

2 large handfuls of mint leaves
1 large handful of coriander leaves
2 garlic cloves
2 green chillis, deseeded and chopped
1 teaspoon finely grated ginger
1 teaspoon honey (optional)
1 tablespoon lemon juice
3 tablespoons extra-virgin olive oil

RAITA

½ Lebanese cucumber
200 g coconut yoghurt (page 84)
½ teaspoon ground cumin
½ teaspoon ground coriander
1 tablespoon chopped mint leaves

INDIAN SPICE MARINADE

2 ½ teaspoons coriander seeds
2 ½ teaspoons cumin seeds
2 ½ teaspoons sea salt
3 teaspoons turmeric
2 ½ teaspoons garam masala
¼ teaspoon chilli powder (or to taste)
3 garlic cloves, grated
1 ½ tablespoons finely grated ginger

There is something so uniquely Australian about lamb chops on the barbecue that always brings a smile to my face. In the olden days, we would team them with some tomato sauce, but these days I love to have this mouth-watering mint chutney as the accompaniment, as it brightens up the dish and has the most tantalising flavour. Mint and lamb are a match made in heaven.

To make the crispy curry leaves, melt the coconut oil in a frying pan over medium heat. Cooking in batches of two sprigs at a time, fry the leaves for 4–5 seconds until crisp. Remove with a slotted spoon and drain on paper towel. Season with salt and set aside.

To make the mint chutney, place the mint, coriander, garlic, chilli, ginger and honey (if using) in a food processor and blend until finely chopped. Add the lemon juice, olive oil and 1 tablespoon of water and continue to blend to a fine paste. Add a little more olive oil if it's too thick. Season with salt.

To make the raita, cut the cucumber in half lengthways and use a teaspoon to scrape out the seeds, then finely dice the cucumber. Combine the cucumber with the yoghurt, cumin, coriander and mint in a bowl and season to taste with salt.

To make the Indian spice marinade, toast the coriander and cumin seeds in a frying pan over medium heat for 1–2 minutes until fragrant. Remove from the heat and allow to cool, then grind in a spice grinder or using a mortar and pestle. Mix the ground spices with the remaining marinade ingredients in a large bowl.

Add the lamb chops to the marinade. Massage the marinade into the lamb chops until well coated. Cover the bowl with plastic wrap and refrigerate for 2 hours or, for best results, overnight.

Heat the coconut oil in a frying pan over medium heat. Cook the lamb, turning occasionally, until browned and cook to your liking (6–7 minutes for medium–rare). Set aside to rest for 5 minutes.

Place the lamb on a large platter and pour over the pan juices. Serve with the mint chutney, raita and lemon wedges on the side, then sprinkle over some toasted cumin seeds. Garnish with the crispy curry leaves.

VIETNAMESE BEEF TARTARE

SERVES 4

1 × 450 g beef eye fillet, cut into
very small dice
2 red Asian shallots, finely chopped
2 kaffir lime leaves, finely chopped
1 tablespoon finely chopped
coriander leaves
sea salt
1 handful of bean sprouts
chilli powder, to serve (optional)

GINGER MAYONNAISE

1 teaspoon finely grated ginger
100 g (⅓ cup) Mayonnaise (page 292)

DRESSING

1 tablespoon finely grated ginger
1 tablespoon finely chopped
coriander roots and stalks
3 garlic cloves, finely chopped
1 long red chilli, deseeded
and chopped
80 ml (⅓ cup) lime juice
2 tablespoons tamari or
coconut aminos*
1 tablespoon fish sauce
1 tablespoon finely chopped
lemongrass, pale part only
1 teaspoon sesame oil
80 ml (⅓ cup) extra-virgin olive oil

SALAD

2 long red chillies, deseeded and
thinly sliced
1 handful of Thai basil leaves
1 handful of mint leaves
1 handful of coriander leaves
1 handful of Vietnamese mint leaves
2 tablespoons chopped, toasted
almonds (activated if possible*)

* See Glossary

Beef tartare is a dish that I believe everyone should try at least once. And this version may just be your ticket to enjoying raw beef at home. For me, raw beef dishes like this are a favourite to make as they can be on the table in less than 10 minutes and are perfect when it is 30°C plus outside. If you can remember to eat mainly cold raw foods in summer and comforting warming stews, braises and soups in winter, then you are eating to the temperature conditions, which is often overlooked when it comes to health.

To make the ginger mayonnaise, place the ginger and mayonnaise in a small bowl and mix well. Set aside until needed.

To make the dressing, combine all the ingredients in the jug of a blender and blend until smooth. Set aside.

Place the diced beef, shallot, lime leaves, coriander and half the dressing in a bowl and mix well. Taste and season with salt, if needed.

Place all the salad ingredients in another bowl and gently toss to combine.

Divide the beef tartare among serving plates and add the bean sprouts, salad, a spoonful of ginger mayonnaise and a drizzle of the remaining dressing. Sprinkle on a little chilli powder (if desired) and serve.

TIP

You can use shichimi togarashi (see Glossary) in place of chilli powder and macadamia oil instead of olive oil in the dressing, if you prefer.

TIP
The pastry dough is soft so it's best
to work fast when lining the pies.

CURRY BEEF PIES

SERVES 4

3 tablespoons coconut oil or
   good-quality animal fat*
1 onion, finely chopped
1 carrot, finely diced
1 celery stalk, finely diced
2 garlic cloves, finely chopped
200 g canned whole peeled
   tomatoes or 2 tomatoes, chopped
1 red chilli, deseeded and
   finely chopped
2 ½ tablespoons curry powder
800 g beef mince
sea salt and freshly ground
   black pepper
500 ml (2 cups) Beef Bone Broth
   (page 282)
2 ½ tablespoons coconut cream
2 tablespoons tapioca flour*
1 egg yolk

PASTRY

60 g (½ cup) almond meal, sifted
50 g coconut flour, sifted
40 g tapioca flour*
½ teaspoon fine sea salt
120 g lard, chilled, cut into
   2.5 cm dice
65 ml ice-cold water
½ teaspoon apple cider vinegar
1 egg

* See Glossary

Yes! We have managed to create a low-carb version of one of the most delicious recipes in the world: the curry beef pie. Feel free to play around with this concept to make a Mexican or Moroccan version, or you may want to do a simple steak and kidney pie. Also try other toppings, such as pumpkin, kohlrabi or celeriac mash.

To make the pastry, combine the almond meal, coconut flour, tapioca flour and salt in a large bowl. Add the lard and, using your fingertips, gently rub it in until the mixture resembles fine crumbs with a few larger pieces. In a separate bowl, whisk together the water, vinegar and egg. Pour over the dry ingredients and mix well to form a soft and slightly sticky dough. Turn the pastry out onto a clean work surface and gently shape into a ball. Cover with plastic wrap and chill in the fridge for at least 1 hour.

Melt the oil or fat in a saucepan over medium heat. Add the onion, carrot and celery and cook, stirring occasionally, for 8 minutes until the vegetables are softened. Add the garlic, tomato and chilli and cook for 3 minutes until the tomato starts to break down. Stir in the curry powder and cook for 1 minute until fragrant, then add the beef mince and cook, stirring to break up any lumps, for 8 minutes until browned. Season with salt and pepper. Pour in the broth and coconut cream, turn the heat down to low and gently simmer for 1 hour.

Mix the tapioca flour with 2 tablespoons of cold water to make a slurry. Stir into the mince mixture, bring to the boil and cook for 2–3 minutes to thicken. Remove from the heat and allow to cool completely.

Preheat the oven to 180°C.

Spoon the curried mince into four ramekins, about 10 cm in diameter.

To make an egg wash, place the egg yolk, 1 tablespoon of water and a pinch of salt in a bowl and whisk to combine. Set aside.

Roll out the pastry between two sheets of baking paper, flipping it over occasionally, until 3 mm thick. Place in the freezer for 20 minutes to firm up again. Peel off the top layer of paper and, using a 10 cm round cutter, cut out four pastry discs. (Cover leftover pastry in plastic wrap and store for up to 3 months in the freezer or 1 week in the fridge.)

Place a pastry disc on each ramekin and gently press round the rim to seal the edge. Lightly brush the pastry with the egg wash and sprinkle on a little salt. Place the pies on a baking tray and transfer to the oven. Bake for 25–30 minutes until the tops are golden and the filling is heated through.

SIRLOIN STEAK WITH FURIKAKE SEASONING, BONITO AIOLI AND GREENS

SERVES 4

4 × 220 g sirloin steaks,
  at room temperature
melted coconut oil or good-quality
  animal fat*, for brushing
sea salt and freshly ground
  black pepper
1 bunch of English spinach
  (about 140 g), trimmed
baby shiso leaves, to serve
  (optional)

SESAME SAUCE

2 teaspoons white miso paste
2 teaspoons coconut sugar
  (optional)
2 tablespoons hulled tahini
2 teaspoons tamari or
  coconut aminos*
2 tablespoons apple cider vinegar
½ teaspoon sesame oil

FURIKAKE SEASONING

2 nori sheets*, torn or snipped
  into 3 cm pieces
1 ½ teaspoons chilli flakes
2 teaspoons sea salt
3 tablespoons bonito flakes*
pinch of coconut sugar (optional)
1 ½ tablespoons sesame seeds,
  toasted

BONITO AIOLI

3 tablespoons bonito flakes*
150 g Aioli (page 280)

* See Glossary

I encourage everyone to eat some form of seaweed weekly, if not daily, as it is one of the most sustainable foods on the planet and nutritionally has so much going for it. Here, we have included seaweed in the form of furikake – a seaweed, salt, bonito (dried tuna) and sesame seed mixture – and teamed it with grilled steak, some green veg and aioli, but please also try it with beef liver, seafood or eggs to see how delicious and versatile it really is.

To make the sesame sauce, combine the miso, 80 ml (⅓ cup) of water and coconut sugar (if using) in a small saucepan over low heat and gently heat, stirring until the sugar dissolves. Remove from the heat, transfer to a bowl and stir in the tahini, tamari or coconut aminos, vinegar and sesame oil. Add a little more water if the sauce is too thick. Set aside until needed.

To make the furikake seasoning, place the nori, chilli flakes, salt and bonito flakes in a blender and pulse a few times to finely chop the nori. Mix in the sugar (if using) and toasted sesame seeds and set aside until needed.

To make the bonito aioli, mix the bonito flakes and aioli to combine. Set aside until needed.

Preheat the oven to 220°C.

Heat a chargrill pan over medium–high heat. Brush the steak on both sides with a little melted oil or fat, season with salt and pepper and chargrill, turning occasionally, until well browned (4–5 minutes). Transfer the steak to a baking tray and roast until cooked to your liking (2–3 minutes for medium–rare). Cover loosely with foil and rest for 5 minutes.

Meanwhile, bring a saucepan of salted water to the boil. Add the spinach and cook for 30 seconds, then plunge into ice-cold water to stop the cooking process. Drain the spinach and squeeze out the excess water with your hands.

To serve, divide the spinach among serving plates and drizzle over the sesame sauce. Slice the beef and arrange on the plates, add a heaped tablespoon of the bonito aioli and sprinkle some furikake seasoning over the steak and spinach. Finish with some shiso leaves (if using).

4

SIDES

SAUTÉED BROCCOLI WITH SPICY MAYONNAISE

SERVES 4

2 heads of broccoli (about 600 g),
broken into florets
2 tablespoons coconut oil or
good-quality animal fat*
4 garlic cloves, chopped
2 long red chillies, deseeded
and thinly sliced
sea salt and freshly ground
black pepper
1 tablespoon extra-virgin olive oil
lemon juice or apple cider vinegar,
to serve (optional)

SPICY MAYONNAISE

1 tablespoon Sriracha Chilli Sauce
(page 296)
100 g (⅓ cup) Mayonnaise
(page 292)

* See Glossary

Here, in this section, we are stepping up the vegetables and letting them take centre stage. The key to this lifestyle is to keep it simple and fill your plate with low-carb veg, then add good fats and protein in the form of seafood, meat or eggs. With this recipe, you have the veg and the fat component sorted, so you just need to cook up a piece of fish or meat to serve alongside. If you don't have time to make a sriracha sauce, simply add chilli flakes, wasabi, horseradish or your choice of herb to the mayo or, for something extraordinary, stir in some canned tuna.

To make the spicy mayonnaise, place the ingredients in a bowl and mix to combine.

Blanch the broccoli in boiling salted water for about 3 minutes until tender, then immediately plunge into ice-cold water to stop the cooking process. When the broccoli is completely cold, drain well and set aside.

Heat the coconut oil or fat in a wok or large frying pan over medium–high heat. Add the garlic and chilli, swirl around in the pan and cook for 30 seconds until fragrant. Add the broccoli and sauté, tossing occasionally, for 5 minutes until starting to colour. Season with salt and pepper and drizzle over the olive oil.

If you like, squeeze a little lemon juice or pour a splash of vinegar over the sautéed broccoli for extra flavour. Serve with the spicy mayonnaise on the side or drizzled over the broccoli.

MANGALOREAN CUCUMBER SALAD (KHARAM)

SERVES 4

4 Lebanese cucumbers, peeled, deseeded and cut into 2 cm dice
sea salt and freshly ground black pepper
1 small handful of mint leaves, chopped, plus extra to serve
toasted cumin seeds, to serve

SAUCE

1 long red chilli, deseeded and finely chopped, plus extra to serve
½ teaspoon yellow or black mustard seeds
¼ red onion, chopped
1 garlic clove, chopped
2 teaspoons lemon juice
150 ml coconut cream or 150 g coconut yoghurt (page 84)

I love the freshness of this salad and I am sure you will too. The combination of crunchy cucumber with mint, chilli and coconut cream or coconut yoghurt is a wonderful marriage of flavours. This makes the perfect accompaniment to Indian-spiced chicken wings or skewers, a lovely turmeric-flavoured fish or a Middle Eastern–style lamb roast.

Place the cucumber in a bowl and mix with ½ teaspoon of salt. Allow to stand for 10 minutes until the cucumber has leached out some liquid. Drain and set aside.

To make the sauce, place all the ingredients in a blender and blend until smooth.

Transfer the sauce to a bowl, add the cucumber and mint and gently mix to combine. Season with salt and pepper and sprinkle on the cumin seeds, extra chilli and mint.

PICKLED ZUCCHINI WITH TURMERIC

MAKES 1 × 1.5 LITRE JAR

500 g zucchini, thinly sliced
  into rounds
1 onion, thinly sliced
2 tablespoons fine sea salt
500 ml (2 cups) chilled water
500 ml (2 cups) apple cider vinegar
100 g honey
2 teaspoons mustard powder
2 teaspoons yellow mustard seeds
1 teaspoon ground turmeric
1 teaspoon black peppercorns
2 bay leaves
3 flat-leaf parsley sprigs

Pickled zucchini is the perfect recipe to make when you see zucchini at the farmers' market or when you have a surplus in your veggie garden. Good on the side with so many dishes, it goes well with burger patties, Korean dishes and fried eggs or you can place them in a little bowl, add another bowl of fermented vegetables and leave them on the table for the family to add as they please to their meals.

You will need a 1.5 litre preserving jar with an airlock lid for this recipe. Wash the jar and all utensils in very hot water or run them through a hot rinse cycle in the dishwasher.

Place the zucchini, onion, salt and water in a bowl and stir to dissolve the salt. Set aside for about 1 hour until the zucchini is tender.

Meanwhile, combine the remaining ingredients in a bowl and stir well.

Drain the zucchini and onion, pat dry with paper towel, then return to the bowl. Add the vinegar mixture, stir to combine, then transfer to the prepared jar. Seal and refrigerate for 2 days to pickle. Stored in the fridge, the pickles will keep for at least 3 weeks.

WHOLE ROASTED CABBAGE WITH BACON AND ONION BROTH

SERVES 8

80 ml (⅓ cup) lard or good-quality
   animal fat*
2 ½ large onions, chopped
5 rindless bacon rashers, chopped
6 garlic cloves, chopped
1 teaspoon sweet paprika
2 teaspoons thyme leaves, chopped
125 ml (½ cup) white wine
   (such as chardonnay)
1 cabbage (about 1.8 kg), outer
   dark green leaves removed
sea salt and freshly ground
   black pepper
750 ml (3 cups) Chicken Bone
   Broth (page 284)
3 tablespoons apple cider vinegar
1 small handful of flat-leaf parsley
   leaves, chopped

* See Glossary

We all need to embrace getting more veggies into our diet. Oven-roasting whole cabbage is a ridiculously easy and fabulous way to celebrate the integrity and flavour of this humble veg, while saving you a heap of time in the kitchen. For the perfect meal, try serving this with roast pork, pork cutlets or some snags. Any leftovers can be chopped or blended into chicken bone broth (page 284) for the most amazing cabbage soup.

Preheat the oven to 160°C.

Place a large frying pan over medium heat. Add 3 tablespoons of lard or fat, then add the onion and sauté, stirring occasionally, for 8 minutes until softened. Add the bacon and cook for 5–6 minutes until the onion is starting to caramelise. Add the garlic, paprika and thyme and sauté for 30 seconds until fragrant. Add the wine, stir well, and cook until the liquid is almost completely reduced. Set aside.

Place the cabbage in a large casserole dish. Rub the remaining lard or fat over the cabbage and season well with salt and pepper. Add the broth and vinegar, then spoon over the bacon and onion mixture. Cover tightly with a lid or baking paper and roast for 3 ½ hours until the cabbage is cooked through. Increase the oven temperature to 170°C. Remove the lid or paper, ladle some broth over the cabbage and return to the oven to roast for 30 minutes until golden. Sprinkle the parsley over the top and serve.

CAULIFLOWER AND BROCCOLI RICE

SERVES 4–6

½ head of cauliflower (about 600 g),
    roughly chopped
1 head of broccoli (about 300 g),
    roughly chopped
2 tablespoons coconut oil
sea salt and freshly ground
    black pepper

Cauliflower rice has taken off as a wonderful way to get more vegetables into our diet over the last few years, because it is quick to make and nutritious. Here, to add more nutritional goodness to your meals, I have suggested a mix of cauliflower and broccoli. This is perfect in sushi rolls or to serve alongside any curry, stir-fry or braised dish. If you like, you can add some finely chopped garlic, spices or herbs to add extra flavour – mustard seeds and curry leaves with coconut oil or duck fat make this pretty spectacular.

Place the cauliflower and broccoli in the bowl of a food processor and pulse into tiny, fine pieces that look like rice.

Heat the oil in a large frying pan over medium heat. Add the cauliflower and broccoli rice and lightly cook for 4–6 minutes until softened. Season with salt and pepper and serve.

BROCCOMOLE

SERVES 2

100 g broccoli, broken into florets
1 avocado, diced or mashed
¼ red onion, chopped
1 garlic clove, finely diced
1 tablespoon lime juice
½ teaspoon chilli flakes (optional)
1 tablespoon extra-virgin olive oil
1 tablespoon chopped coriander
  leaves
sea salt and freshly ground
  black pepper

TO SERVE

lemon wedges
seeded crackers or sweet potato
  crisps (optional)

Haha! You have to have a laugh when it comes to making up dish titles. Here is the wonderful broccomole, which takes its name from mixing the classic guacamole with broccoli. I prefer to use cooked and chilled broccoli in the mix, but you can use raw broccoli if you choose. This is perfect on bacon chips, or on the side with some eggs, fish, steak, pork or snags. For something a little fun, you can also add some cooked or raw fish and try it as a filling for nori rolls. Feel free to add some toasted seeds, such as sesame or sunflower, for a little more flavour and texture.

Bring a saucepan of salted water to the boil. Add the broccoli and cook for 3 minutes until just tender. Drain, then plunge the broccoli into ice-cold water to stop the cooking process. When the broccoli is completely cold, drain again and shake off any excess water. Chop the cooled broccoli into small pieces and set aside.

Place the avocado, onion, garlic, lime juice, chilli flakes (if using), oil, coriander and broccoli in a serving bowl and mix well. Season with salt and pepper. Serve with the lemon wedges and some seeded crackers or sweet potato crisps, if desired.

TIP

This recipe is the base for Broccomole Fat Bombs on page 54.

BRUSSELS SPROUTS WITH BACON AND GARLIC

SERVES 4

2 tablespoons coconut oil or
    good-quality animal fat*
150 g rindless bacon,
    roughly chopped
500 g brussels sprouts,
    halved lengthways
4 garlic cloves, thinly sliced
375 ml (1 ½ cups) Chicken Bone
    Broth (page 284)
finely grated zest of 1 lemon
chilli flakes, to serve (optional)

* See Glossary

Brussels sprouts and bacon is a very classic culinary marriage that I have been cooking and enjoying for years. This dish may actually be the one that will get your kids enjoying brussels sprouts, but I can't promise anything. Serve this alongside your favourite roast, some grilled fish, meat or sausages.

Heat the oil or fat in a large, heavy-based frying pan over medium heat. Add the bacon and cook, stirring occasionally, for 4–5 minutes until the bacon starts to brown. Add the brussels sprouts and cook for 2–3 minutes until the sprouts start to turn golden brown. Add the garlic and cook for 30 seconds until starting to colour.

Reduce the heat to medium–low. Pour in the chicken broth and cook, stirring occasionally, for 15–20 minutes until the brussels sprouts are tender. Sprinkle on the lemon zest and chilli flakes (if using) and serve.

CAULIFLOWER AND PUMPKIN 'DAL'

SERVES 4–6

80 ml (⅓ cup) coconut oil or
   good-quality animal fat*
20 curry leaves
1 teaspoon yellow or brown
   mustard seeds
1 onion, finely chopped
1 tablespoon finely grated ginger
2 garlic cloves, chopped
500 g peeled butternut pumpkin,
   cut into 1 cm dice
3 teaspoons garam masala
2 teaspoons ground turmeric
2 teaspoons ground cumin
1–2 pinches of cayenne pepper
500 ml (2 cups) Chicken Bone
   Broth (page 284) or water
200 ml coconut cream
1 tablespoon lemon juice
½ head of cauliflower (about 600 g),
   broken into florets
sea salt and freshly ground
   black pepper

* See Glossary

A lot of people, myself included, like to stick to tradition when it comes to preparing certain dishes from particular cuisines. Indian is one of the tricky cuisines for me, as I love Indian food and don't want to compromise on flavour. When I first started converting the Indian recipes I love to paleo, I wondered how I could replace the split peas or lentils in much-loved dal. Still pondering this, I had the good fortune to be in Arnhem Land in the Northern Territory with the Hope For Health team, who are working to create a healthier community. While there, one of the volunteer cooks served up the most amazing dal. I immediately asked to borrow the recipe – and here it is. Serve this alongside any Indian or Sri Lankan dish or simply with some snags.

Heat the oil or fat in a saucepan over medium heat. Add half the curry leaves and the mustard seeds and fry for 10 seconds until the mustard seeds start to pop. Immediately strain through a very fine sieve, reserving the oil or fat. Drain on paper towel and set aside.

Heat the reserved oil or fat in a large frying pan or casserole dish over medium heat. Add the onion and cook, stirring occasionally, for 5 minutes until translucent. Add the ginger, garlic and pumpkin and cook for 1 minute, then stir in the spices and the remaining curry leaves and cook for 30 seconds until fragrant. Pour in the broth, coconut cream and lemon juice, cover with a lid and bring to the boil. Reduce the heat to medium–low and simmer for 10 minutes until the pumpkin is tender.

Meanwhile, place the cauliflower in the bowl of a food processor and pulse into tiny, fine pieces that look like rice.

Stir the cauliflower rice into the simmering pumpkin, cover with the lid and simmer for 10–15 minutes until the cauliflower is cooked through. Season with salt and pepper. Serve with the crispy curry leaves and mustard seeds scattered over the top.

STEAMED CAULIFLOWER PUREE

SERVES 4

1 large head of cauliflower
  (about 1.3 kg), chopped into florets
2 tablespoons coconut oil or
  good-quality animal fat*, melted

HERB OIL

1 tablespoon finely chopped
  flat-leaf parsley leaves
1 tablespoon finely chopped
  dill fronds
3 tablespoons lemon-infused olive
  oil or extra-virgin olive oil
sea salt and freshly ground
  black pepper

* See Glossary

This lovely creamy puree will become a regular part of your cooking repertoire after you have tried it. Fantastic as a replacement for the old faithful mashed potato, the even greater news is that it is so much quicker to cook, it won't elevate your blood-sugar levels and it works a treat with everything from grilled seafood and meat to roasts, sausages, shepherd's and cottage pies, curries and duck confit.

To make the herb oil, combine the parsley, dill and oil in a small bowl and mix well. Season with salt and pepper and set aside until needed.

Fill a saucepan with water and place a steamer with a lid on top. Bring to the boil, place the cauliflower florets in the steamer, cover and steam for 30–35 minutes until the cauliflower is very soft. Place the cauliflower in the bowl of a food processor and process until smooth. Add the oil or fat and blitz again, then season with salt and pepper.

Transfer the cauliflower puree to a serving bowl or plates and drizzle some herb oil over the top.

COCONUT CAULIFLOWER RICE

SERVES 4–6

1 head of cauliflower (about 1 kg),
   roughly chopped
1 tablespoon coconut oil
½ onion, finely chopped
½ teaspoon ground cardamom
   (optional)
½ teaspoon ground cumin (optional)
1 × 400 ml can coconut milk
125 ml (½ cup) Chicken Bone Broth
   (page 284) or water
sea salt and freshly ground
   black pepper
coriander and mint leaves, to serve

Here, I have taken the now-classic cauliflower rice and upped the stakes a little to turn it into coconut cauliflower rice, as some dishes require a side with a little more substance and texture. Use this delicious rice to accompany spiced roasted meats, tagines, curries, soups or anything else you can come up with.

Place the cauliflower in the bowl of a food processor and pulse into tiny, fine pieces that resemble rice.

Heat the oil in a large non-stick frying pan over medium heat. Add the onion and cook for 5 minutes until softened and translucent. Add the spices (if using) and stir for about 10 seconds until fragrant.

Add the cauliflower rice, coconut milk and broth or water to the pan, stir to combine and simmer, stirring occasionally, for 8–10 minutes until the cauliflower rice is cooked through and has thickened slightly. Season with salt and pepper and serve sprinkled with the coriander and mint.

JAPANESE SPINACH SALAD (OHITASHI)

SERVES 2

250 ml (1 cup) cold Dashi Broth
   (page 286)
1 tablespoon tamari or
   coconut aminos*
1 teaspoon coconut sugar (optional)
4 bunches of English spinach
   (about 1 kg), stalks trimmed
   and discarded
2 cm piece of ginger,
   cut into thin matchsticks

TO SERVE

1 spring onion, green part
   thinly sliced
2 tablespoons bonito flakes*
½ teaspoon toasted sesame seeds
sesame oil

* See Glossary

I ate this dish the first time I went to a Japanese restaurant close to 30 years ago – and I can still remember the taste, texture and sheer amazement at how good spinach could be. I have kept this as true to tradition as I could and, to be honest, I don't think there is anything I can do to improve it. When you feel like being Popeye and upping your spinach intake, serve this alongside basically anything: soups, stir-fries, grilled seafood and meat, or raw meat or seafood dishes.

Place the dashi broth, tamari or coconut aminos and coconut sugar (if using) in a small saucepan and heat, stirring, until the broth is warm and the sugar has dissolved. Remove from the heat and set aside until needed.

Blanch the spinach in a large saucepan of boiling salted water for 10 seconds until wilted and bright green. Drain and plunge into iced water to cool completely. Drain again and squeeze out as much excess water as possible.

Fill another small saucepan with water and bring to the boil. Add the ginger and cook for 3 minutes until the ginger is softened slightly. Drain and allow to cool.

Using a bamboo sushi mat and working at the edge closest to you, pack and mould the spinach into a long cylinder shape about 3.5 cm thick and roll up tightly. Carefully unroll and remove the mat. Alternatively, if you don't have a sushi mat, simply shape the spinach into a long 3.5 cm thick cylinder. Use a sharp knife to cut the spinach into 4 cm lengths.

Divide the spinach between serving bowls, ladle over the broth, then finish with the spring onion, ginger, bonito flakes and sesame seeds. Drizzle over a couple of drops of sesame oil and serve.

CUCUMBER AND AVOCADO SALAD WITH GINGER AND SESAME

SERVES 4

4 Lebanese cucumbers,
   halved lengthways and cut into
   1 cm thick pieces
1 avocado, cut into 1 cm dice
2.5 cm piece of ginger,
   cut into matchsticks
2 spring onions, thinly sliced
1 large handful of mint leaves
1 large handful of coriander leaves
1–2 teaspoons toasted
   sesame seeds

DRESSING

3 tablespoons apple cider vinegar
1 teaspoon honey (optional)
2 garlic cloves, finely grated
1 red Asian shallot, finely chopped
80 ml (⅓ cup) extra-virgin olive oil
2 teaspoons sesame oil
sea salt and freshly ground
   black pepper

You have to love a salad that has delicious and nourishing fat worked into it. And that is exactly what we have here with this simple and satisfying side dish. You don't need much time to put this one together, and if you want to turn it into a proper meal, simply add cooked prawns or chicken, sliced raw seafood or cold hard-boiled eggs to bulk it out a little or a lot.

To make the dressing, combine all the ingredients in a bowl and mix well. Set aside.

Place the cucumber, avocado, ginger, spring onion and herbs in a bowl, add the dressing and gently toss to coat the salad. Arrange on a serving dish, sprinkle over the sesame seeds and serve.

CURLY ENDIVE AND WALNUT SALAD

SERVES 4

½ curly endive, leaves separated
and torn
2–3 roma tomatoes,
cut into wedges
35 g (⅓ cup) walnuts (activated if
possible*), toasted and chopped
2 spring onions, greens part cut
into thin strips and soaked in
cold water to curl, white parts
thinly sliced
2 tablespoons red wine vinegar
or apple cider vinegar
½ teaspoon Dijon mustard
3 tablespoons extra-virgin olive oil
sea salt and freshly ground
black pepper

* See Glossary

Curly endive contains good levels of vitamins A and K and folate. A bitter green leaf that has long been appreciated in Europe as a delicacy, it adds a wonderful texture and piquancy to salads. You can also lightly cook it with some cinnamon and drizzle with olive oil and lemon juice or add it to your favourite soups. If the flavour in this salad is a little overpowering for the whole family, mix the endive leaves with less strongly flavoured lettuces.

Place the endive, tomato, walnuts and spring onion in a large bowl. Set aside.

To make the dressing, combine the vinegar, mustard and olive oil in a small bowl, season with salt and pepper and whisk well to combine.

Pour the dressing over the salad and gently toss to coat. Season with some salt and pepper and serve in a large salad bowl or on a platter.

TOMATO AND AVOCADO SALAD

SERVES 4

4–5 heirloom tomatoes, sliced
sea salt and freshly ground
    black pepper
2 garlic cloves, finely chopped
½ red onion, thinly sliced
1 avocado, cut into 2 cm pieces
1 handful of mixed herb leaves
    (such as flat-leaf parsley, oregano
    and basil), roughly chopped
2–3 tablespoons red wine vinegar
    or apple cider vinegar
80 ml (⅓ cup) extra-virgin olive oil

You know summer has arrived when tomato season is in full swing. When tomatoes are super ripe and full of flavour, there is no better time to add them to your diet. This wonderful salad really makes the most of them.

Place the tomato on a platter, sprinkle on some salt and pepper, then scatter over the garlic. Arrange the slices of red onion on the tomato, then add a layer of avocado and herbs.

To make the dressing, whisk the vinegar and olive oil in a small bowl until well combined.

Drizzle the dressing over the tomato salad, sprinkle on a little more salt and pepper, if desired, and serve.

ICEBERG WEDGE SALAD WITH BACON AND EGG

SERVES 6

1 teaspoon coconut oil or
    good-quality fat*
4 rindless bacon rashers,
    cut into small dice
1 large iceberg lettuce, cored
    and cut into 6 wedges
4 hard-boiled eggs, chopped
100 g (⅓ cup) Aioli or Mayonnaise
    (pages 280 and 292)
1 small handful of flat-leaf parsley,
    roughly chopped
extra-virgin olive oil, to serve

DRESSING

3 tablespoons apple cider vinegar
1 tablespoon honey (optional)
1 teaspoon Dijon mustard
sea salt and freshly ground
    black pepper

* See Glossary

Sometimes you just need a good iceberg salad to quench your thirst, especially when it's hot outside. The fresh crispness of a cold iceberg lettuce is very hard to beat. It may not be the most nutrient-dense of lettuces or leafy greens, but it makes for a welcome change. We love to add boiled eggs and bacon, smoked trout or even leftover roast chicken, and then use a mayonnaise, tahini or simple vinaigrette to dress it.

Heat the coconut oil or fat in a frying pan over medium heat. Add the bacon and cook for 5–8 minutes until golden and crisp. Strain the bacon fat from the pan into a bowl and reserve. Set the cooked bacon aside, keeping warm.

To make the dressing, combine the vinegar, honey (if using) and mustard with the reserved bacon fat and mix well. Season with a little salt and pepper. Keep warm.

Place the iceberg wedges on a platter, then spoon on the dressing. Scatter over the bacon and egg, then drizzle on the aioli or mayonnaise, sprinkle over the parsley and finish with a splash of olive oil.

JERUSALEM ARTICHOKES WITH BACON AND GARLIC

SERVES 4

1 kg Jerusalem artichokes, skin on,
    cut into 2.5 cm dice
150 g rindless bacon, cut into
    2 cm pieces
3 rosemary sprigs, roughly chopped
1 garlic bulb, cloves separated,
    skin on
3 tablespoons goose fat or
    good-quality animal fat*
sea salt and freshly ground
    black pepper
2 tablespoons finely snipped chives

* See Glossary

When it comes to taste, I don't think there is a better vegetable in the world than the Jerusalem artichoke. I still remember the first time I ever tried one roasted in duck fat. It blew me away at how deliciously moreish it was: nutty, earthy and sweet all at the same time. Jerusalem artichokes are also known as 'sunchokes' and are a wonderful form of prebiotic that your gut will love. Be warned though: some people experience flatulence when they consume these tasty morsels.

Preheat the oven to 180°C. Line a large roasting tin with baking paper.

Place the artichokes, bacon, rosemary, garlic and fat in the prepared tin and mix to coat the artichokes in the fat. Season with salt and pepper and roast for 35–45 minutes until the artichokes are tender inside and crispy on the outside. Season with salt and pepper, if needed, sprinkle over the chives and serve.

SAUTÉED KALE WITH BACON

SERVES 4

1 bunch of curly kale (about 350 g)
1 tablespoon coconut oil or
   good-quality animal fat*
3 rindless bacon rashers,
   cut into 1 cm pieces
3 garlic cloves, thinly sliced
3 tablespoons Chicken or Beef Bone
   Broth (pages 284 and 282)
   or water
sea salt and freshly ground
   black pepper

* See Glossary

As a family, we love our greens and they feature at every meal, whether it is breakfast, lunch or dinner. The greens we particularly love include kale, silverbeet, spinach, broccoli, zucchini, asparagus, snow peas, cucumber, lettuce, okra and herbs. A great way to get the kids to enjoy greens as a main part of each meal is to add some bacon when cooking or serving, as it imparts a wonderful flavour and some good fats, too. Give this a whirl and see how much your family loves it.

Wash the kale thoroughly in cold water and pat dry. Remove and discard the tough central stems, then cut the leaves into smaller pieces.

Heat the oil or fat in a large frying pan over medium heat, add the bacon and cook for 3–4 minutes until lightly golden. Stir in the garlic and cook for 30 seconds until softened and starting to colour. Add the kale leaves and broth or water and continue to cook, stirring occasionally, for 3–4 minutes until the kale is slightly wilted. Season with salt and pepper, then arrange the sautéed kale and bacon on a platter and serve.

FENNEL, WATERCRESS AND HERB SALAD WITH SHALLOT DRESSING

SERVES 4

1 large fennel bulb, trimmed,
  fronds reserved
1 large handful of watercress
1 handful of mint leaves
1 handful of dill fronds

SHALLOT DRESSING
1 French shallot, finely diced
3 tablespoons apple cider vinegar
1 teaspoon Dijon mustard
80 ml (⅓ cup) extra-virgin olive oil
sea salt and freshly ground
  black pepper

I am a huge fan of fennel and believe it is an underutilised vegetable. When it is in season I roast, braise and ferment it, and use it raw as I've done here. This easy yet delicious fennel salad deserves a place on every dinner table. Simply serve it alongside some grilled fish or roasted meat.

Mint pairs perfectly with fennel and is a very good place to start, but feel free to play around with other herbs of your choice. You may also like to add some seeds or nuts, such as walnuts, almonds or macadamias, for a bit of crunch.

Using a mandoline or sharp knife, thinly shave the fennel.

Place the shaved fennel, watercress, herbs and fennel fronds in a large bowl and set aside while you prepare the dressing.

To make the dressing, place all the ingredients in a small bowl and whisk to combine.

Pour only enough dressing over the salad to coat, then gently toss through. Check for seasoning and add more salt and pepper if needed.

Arrange the fennel salad on a large platter and drizzle over a little more dressing, if desired.

TIP
Any leftover dressing can be stored in a sealed jar in the fridge for up to 2 weeks.

WITLOF, PARSLEY AND PINE NUT SALAD WITH ANCHOVY DRESSING

SERVES 4

2 witlof, trimmed and leaves
   separated
¼ bunch of curly endive
   (about 120 g), leaves separated
   and roughly torn
30 g pine nuts, toasted
3 tablespoons roughly chopped
   flat-leaf parsley leaves

DRESSING

4 anchovy fillets, finely chopped
2 garlic cloves, finely grated
2 tablespoons apple cider vinegar
3 tablespoons extra-virgin olive oil
sea salt and freshly ground
   black pepper

You can see from the other recipes in this book that I have included quite a few bitter ingredients. The reason for this is that bitterness expands the palate and helps stop sweet cravings. If you have a sugar addiction, start adding bitter, astringent and sour foods to your diet.

This easy-to-make salad of crisp and slightly bitter pale green witlof and curly endive leaves is so delicious with its anchovy dressing. You can also use this versatile dressing on grilled broccolini, lamb cutlets or seafood.

To make the dressing, place all the ingredients in a bowl and mix to combine.

Arrange the witlof and curly endive on a platter and pour the dressing over the leaves. Sprinkle on the pine nuts and parsley and serve.

ZUCCHINI AND MINT SALAD

SERVES 4

2 tablespoons coconut oil or
   good-quality animal fat*
3 garlic cloves, thinly sliced
3 zucchini, cut on the diagonal
   into 1 cm slices
sea salt and freshly ground
   black pepper
1 ½ tablespoons apple cider vinegar
3 tablespoons extra-virgin olive oil
2 tablespoons pine nuts, toasted
2 tablespoons currants
1 small handful of flat-leaf parsley
   leaves, finely chopped
1 small handful of mint leaves

* See Glossary

Here is another wonderful salad you can put together in a matter of minutes when zucchini is at its peak in summer. If you'd like to turn this into a meal, add some raw tuna, cooked prawns or roast chicken.

Heat 1 tablespoon of coconut oil or fat in a large frying pan over medium heat. Add the garlic and cook for 30 seconds until just starting to colour. Immediately remove the garlic from the pan and set aside.

Melt the remaining coconut oil or fat in the same pan over medium-high heat. Add the zucchini in batches and fry for 1 minute on each side until golden brown and just cooked through. You don't want to overcook the zucchini, as it will become mushy. Season with salt and pepper and set aside until needed.

Mix the garlic, vinegar and olive oil in a small bowl and season with salt and pepper.

Toss the zucchini with the pine nuts, currants, parsley, mint and garlic dressing to combine. Arrange on a platter and serve warm or at room temperature.

5

TREATS

ALMOND AND CHOCOLATE FAT BOMBS

MAKES 9

CHOCOLATE LAYER

1 ½ tablespoons raw cacao powder
1 tablespoon coconut cream
3 tablespoons coconut oil
⅛ teaspoon vanilla powder
¼ teaspoon ground cinnamon
⅛ teaspoon liquid stevia
    (or 1 ½ teaspoons xylitol or honey)

ALMOND LAYER

3 tablespoons coconut oil
100 g almond butter
¼ teaspoon ground cinnamon
⅛ teaspoon liquid stevia
    (or 1 ½ teaspoons xylitol or honey)

COCONUT CREAM LAYER

3 tablespoons coconut oil
45 g (½ cup) desiccated coconut
2 tablespoons coconut cream
⅛ teaspoon liquid stevia
    (or 1 ½ teaspoons xylitol or honey)

TOPPING

70 g Nut Muesli (page 294)

You are going to love making these delicious fat bombs (which are dairy free, of course). They make for a wonderful snack on camping and road trips and are full of good-quality fats, so you will feel extremely satisfied after a bite or two and will not be tempted to eat too many.

Line a 12-cup standard muffin tin with nine paper cases.

To make the chocolate layer, combine the cacao powder, coconut cream, coconut oil, vanilla, cinnamon and stevia in a small saucepan and stir over low heat until the coconut oil is just melted and there are no lumps. Remove from the heat, allow to cool to lukewarm, then stir well and evenly divide between the paper cases. Place in the fridge to set for 20 minutes.

When the chocolate layer is set, make the almond layer. Melt the coconut oil in a small saucepan over low heat. Stir in the almond butter, cinnamon and stevia and cook for 1 minute until warmed through. Remove from the heat and cool to lukewarm. Stir and pour over the chocolate layer. Return to the fridge to set for another 30 minutes.

To make the coconut cream layer, melt the coconut oil in a saucepan. Remove from the heat and mix together with the remaining ingredients until smooth.

Spoon the coconut cream layer evenly over the almond layer in each paper case, then sprinkle on 1 tablespoon of nut muesli. Return the fat bombs to the fridge to set for 30 minutes before serving.

TIP

If you want to make this recipe keto friendly, omit the currants from the nut muesli topping.

GREEN JUICE POPSICLES

MAKES 8

¼ bunch of silverbeet (about 220 g),
   stems trimmed
2 green apples, cored
1 handful of mint leaves and stalks
2 celery stalks
1 Lebanese cucumber
½ lemon, peeled and chopped
2.5 cm piece of ginger,
   peeled and chopped

When summer hits and you're craving an icy pole, these green juice popsicles are just what the doctor ordered. Obviously, they are not going to be sweet, as they are mainly vegetable based, but you can add some delicious mint and even a little MCT oil (see Note page 255) or coconut oil for extra fat (some people like to add a bit of chicken bone broth, too). For something different, try freezing the chai on page 260 for a flavoursome ice cream.

Juice all the ingredients.

Pour the juice into eight 80 ml (⅓ cup) icy-pole moulds and place in the freezer for 1 hour. After 1 hour, insert an icy-pole stick in each mould. Return to the freezer for 4–8 hours until completely frozen.

TIP
To flavour your kombucha, after bottling, add some fruit or spices of your choice and allow the kombucha to sit at room temperature for a day or two to ferment further. This second fermentation produces more bubbles and makes the kombucha fizzy. I recommend adding sliced ginger, apple and cinnamon or fruits such as mangoes, peaches, plums and berries.

KOMBUCHA GRANITA

MAKES 3 LITRES

3 litres filtered water
90 g raw sugar or coconut sugar
35 g (½ cup) black tea leaves
125 ml (½ cup) pre-made kombucha
   (from a previous batch or
   a store-bought bottle)
1 SCOBY
mint leaves, to serve

I have been making kombucha for the last 25 years and I love how it packs a probiotic punch. You can make your own kombucha pretty easily once you have a SCOBY (Symbiotic Colony of Bacteria and Yeast), or you can use a pre-made bottled version from a health-food store (always make sure you buy one with minimal sugar).

You will need a wide-mouth 4 litre glass jar and four 1 litre glass bottles with screw-top lids for this recipe. To sterilise the jars, wash them in very hot, soapy water and run them through a hot rinse cycle in your dishwasher. If you don't have a dishwasher, boil the jars in a large saucepan of boiling water for 10 minutes, then transfer to a baking tray and place in a 150°C oven for 10 minutes, or until completely dry.

Bring 750 ml of filtered water to the boil in a stainless steel saucepan. Add the sugar and stir until dissolved. Remove from the heat and add the tea leaves. Set aside to cool completely.

Pour the sweet tea through a fine strainer into the sterilised 4 litre jar. Add the pre-made kombucha, the SCOBY and the remaining water. Cover the top of your jar with muslin and secure with a rubber band.

Leave the jar in a warm, dark place with a temperature of 18–28°C for 8 days. (On top of the fridge works well or, if you live in a colder climate, you can use a heating mat like those used for seedlings.) As your kombucha ferments, a new SCOBY will form, attached to the original one, expanding to the width of your container.

After 8 days of fermenting, taste your kombucha. It should be slightly sweet and sour, with a hint of tea. If it's too sweet, leave it to ferment for a few more days. If you're happy with it, use clean hands to remove the SCOBY and separate it from the new one. You now have two SCOBYs, which you can use to make more kombucha (or you can give one to a friend who is interested in making their own). If you don't wish to make another batch of kombucha straight away, store the SCOBYs in a solution of sweetened tea on the bench. Don't put them in the fridge or they will go into hibernation.

Transfer the kombucha to the sterilised glass bottles, leaving about 1.5 cm free at the top. Screw the lids tightly in place and transfer to the fridge.

To make the granita, pour 1–2 litres of kombucha into a deep tray, cover and freeze for a few hours. Run a fork through the frozen kombucha to create ice shavings.

Spoon the granita into glasses and serve topped with the mint.

BLACKBERRY–COCONUT FAT BOMBS

MAKES 12

150 g coconut butter, softened
100 ml coconut oil, softened
100 g fresh or frozen blackberries
⅛ teaspoon liquid stevia
   (or 1 ½ teaspoons xylitol)
¼ teaspoon vanilla powder
shredded coconut, for rolling

You will have noticed that bliss balls have become very popular over the last few years, but most are made with dates or dried figs, so are just a sugar bomb in disguise – and that is not great for blood-sugar levels. So, here, instead of the dried fruit–filled bliss balls, I share a low-carb version that is full of good fats.

Place the coconut butter, oil, blackberries, stevia and vanilla in the bowl of a food processor and blend until smooth.

Divide the coconut butter mixture into walnut-sized portions and, between slightly wet palms, roll into balls. Roll the balls in the shredded coconut and set on a plate or tray. Cover and refrigerate for 20 minutes to set before serving. Store in an airtight container in the fridge for up to 2 weeks.

TIP
You can also use fresh or frozen raspberries, strawberries, blueberries or mixed berries.

KETO CHOCOLATE AND COCONUT BITES

MAKES 15–20

3 tablespoons raw cacao
   powder, sifted
1 tablespoon carob powder
150 g cacao butter, chopped
2 tablespoons coconut oil
¼ teaspoon vanilla powder
½ teaspoon liquid stevia
3 tablespoons coconut cream
small pinch of sea salt
100 g coconut flakes

What more is there to say than YUMMO when it comes to these tasty little morsels?

Grease a mini muffin tin or chocolate mould tray.

Combine the cacao powder, carob powder, cacao butter, coconut oil, vanilla and stevia in a heatproof bowl over a saucepan of simmering water. Make sure the bowl doesn't touch the water (or it will overheat). Stir with a metal spoon until smooth and the butters are just melted. Remove from the heat and stir through the coconut cream. Allow to cool to lukewarm, then stir in the salt and coconut flakes. Spoon the mixture evenly into the prepared muffin tins and place in the fridge for 1 hour until firm.

Remove the tins from the fridge, tap the base of each tin on the bench a couple of times, then flip over to remove the bites. They should pop out easily, but if they don't, try tapping the tin again on the bench. Store in an airtight container in the fridge.

TIP
You can also add a couple of drops of food-grade essential oil to these bites, such as orange or spearmint. Food-grade essential oils can be purchased from health-food stores or online.

RASPBERRY AND COCONUT CREAMS

MAKES 40–45

150 g frozen raspberries, thawed
¼ teaspoon liquid stevia
   (or 2 teaspoons xylitol or honey)
1 tablespoon powdered gelatine

COCONUT CREAM LAYER

120 ml coconut cream
¼ teaspoon liquid stevia
   (or 2 teaspoons xylitol or honey)
1 tablespoon powdered gelatine

You are going to love making these treats for yourself and the whole family, as they are relatively simple to prepare, are delicious and look pretty awesome. They are also full of good fats and gut-healing gelatine, as well as antioxidants from the berries.

Combine the raspberries and 3 tablespoons of water in a blender and pulse a couple of times to form a puree. Don't over-pulse, as you don't want to blend the tiny raspberry seeds (this will make your jelly grainy). Strain through a fine sieve into a small saucepan. (Discard the leftover raspberry pulp.) Stir in the stevia, sprinkle over the gelatine and stir until the gelatine is incorporated. Allow to stand for 5 minutes.

Place the pan over medium–low heat and cook, stirring constantly, for 5 minutes until the raspberry mixture is completely smooth. Make sure you don't boil the mixture.

Pour the raspberry mixture into silicone ice-cube trays or chocolate moulds until half full, then immediately place in the freezer for 15 minutes to set.

Meanwhile, to make the coconut cream layer, place the coconut cream and stevia in a small saucepan and stir to combine. Sprinkle the powdered gelatine over 2 tablespoons of water and allow to stand for 5 minutes to bloom, then stir the gelatine through the hot coconut cream mixture to combine. Cook, stirring constantly, over medium–low heat for 5 minutes until completely smooth. Do not allow the mixture to boil. Set aside to cool to lukewarm.

Once the raspberry jellies have set, pour the cooled coconut mixture into the ice-cube tray or chocolate moulds until filled to the top and immediately place in the freezer for a further 15 minutes until set.

Remove the jellies from the moulds and store in an airtight jar. They will keep for a few weeks in the fridge.

TURMERIC AND MACADAMIA CHOCOLATE BARK

SERVES 4–6

140 g cacao butter

3 tablespoons coconut milk
    powder, sifted

1 teaspoon ground turmeric

⅛ teaspoon liquid stevia
    (or 1 ½ teaspoons xylitol or honey)

1 vanilla pod, seeds scraped

¼ teaspoon ground cinnamon

2 tablespoons cashew or
    almond butter

120 g macadamia nuts (activated
    if possible*), roughly chopped

pinch of sea salt

* See Glossary

This treat is full of good fats and medicinal spices and that, for me, is a double thumbs-up. When you compare this type of treat made from all-natural ingredients to store-bought chocolate bars full of additives and preservatives, if you are going to indulge you really owe it to yourself to make your own.

Place the cacao butter in a heatproof bowl over a saucepan of gently simmering water and stir with a metal spoon until melted and smooth. (Ensure the bowl fits snugly over the saucepan and does not come into contact with the water in the pan.) Remove from the heat, add the coconut milk powder, turmeric, stevia, vanilla pod and seeds, cinnamon and nut butter and whisk until the mixture is shiny and smooth.

Line a 28 cm × 23 cm tray with baking paper. Pour on the cacao butter mixture and spread out with a palette knife or spatula to form an even layer 3–5 mm thick. Evenly sprinkle over the macadamias and salt. Transfer to the freezer and chill for 30 minutes, or until set.

Peel the solid bark off the paper and cut or break into pieces. Serve or store in an airtight container in the fridge for up to 3 weeks.

6

DRINKS

APPLE CIDER VINEGAR WATER

SERVES 4

2–3 tablespoons apple cider vinegar
1 litre (4 cups) warm filtered water

Having a daily spoonful or two of raw organic apple cider vinegar is a good habit to get into, as that little hit of tartness helps in so many ways. The ingestion of apple cider vinegar has been said to help with skin irritations, candida overgrowth, acid reflux and other digestive problems, as well as sore throats, inflamed sinuses, heart problems and blood-sugar issues. A lot of people drink it to help them lose weight, but if you continue to eat the same, standard Australian diet, then no amount of apple cider vinegar is going to help. However, the inclusion of apple cider vinegar in a low-carb paleo diet is worth a shot (pardon the pun).

Stir the apple cider vinegar into the warm water and drink, on an empty stomach, in the first 30 minutes after waking. Food or other drinks should not be consumed for 30–60 minutes.

WATER WITH LEMON AND SALT

SERVES 4

1 litre (4 cups) warm filtered water
2 tablespoons lemon juice
2 teaspoons sea salt

This is another drink you may wish to add to your daily or weekly routine, or alternate with the apple cider vinegar water on page 250. The inclusion of lemon and good-quality salt like Himalayan or sea salt in filtered water can help fight inflammation and add much-needed trace minerals. Drinking this also boosts the immune system through the addition of vitamin C from the lemon juice and can help to detox as well. This amazing little concoction is great for skin, helps with sleep issues and is thought to help stabilise blood-sugar levels.

Combine the warm water, lemon juice and salt and stir until the salt has dissolved. Drink, on an empty stomach, in the first 30 minutes after waking. Food or other drinks should not be consumed for 30–60 minutes.

GREEN JUICE WITH MCT OIL

SERVES 2–4

½ bunch of English spinach
   (about 60 g), trimmed
   (or baby spinach, kale
   or silverbeet)
2 green apples, cored
1 small handful of mint leaves
   and stalks
1 small handful of flat-leaf parsley
   leaves and stalks
1 Lebanese cucumber
1 lime, peeled and chopped
4 cm piece of ginger,
   peeled and chopped
2 tablespoons coconut oil or
   MCT oil (see Note)
ice cubes (optional)

If you feel like having a green juice, I strongly urge you to add a shot of MCT oil. Now, a lot of green juices you buy are full of fruit – which is essentially a sugar bomb – so I have included a low-sugar version for you here, as I know some people love to have juice daily. Just remember to go easy on the sweet fruit. For more information on MCT oil, see the Note below.

Juice the spinach, apple, mint, parsley, cucumber, lime and ginger. Pour in the oil and stir well.

Pour the juice into glasses and serve with ice, if desired.

NOTE

MCT stands for medium-chain triglycerides, a special type of saturated fatty acid that is easily digested to provide fast, sustained energy. MCT oil is believed to improve cognitive function and help maintain a healthy body weight. It's also said to be great for balancing hormones, regulating blood sugar and supporting gut health, and to have antibacterial and antifungal properties. MCT oil can be found in health-food stores or online – use coconut oil instead if you can't find it.

TURMERIC, LEMON AND GINGER JUICE WITH MCT OIL

SERVES 2

500 ml (2 cups) coconut water
5 cm piece of fresh turmeric or
   1 teaspoon ground turmeric
3 cm piece of ginger, sliced
1 tablespoon coconut oil or
   MCT oil (see Note page 255)
juice of ½ lemon
½ teaspoon sea salt (optional)

This has to be one of my favourite drinks of all time. The mixture of lemon, turmeric and ginger with a hit of coconut or MCT oil has all the makings of a very powerful and potent medicinal drink. You can prepare this a couple of ways: either pop the lemon flesh, turmeric and ginger in a juicer or you can hand squeeze the lemon and then blitz the turmeric, ginger, water, lemon juice and oil in a blender. If you find the lemon a little strong, you can use grapefruit or orange juice instead.

Place the coconut water, turmeric, ginger and oil in a blender and blend until smooth. Strain into a jug (discard the leftover ginger and turmeric pulp). Stir through the lemon juice and salt (if using), pour into glasses and serve.

FAT BOMB GREEN SMOOTHIE

SERVES 2–4

400 ml coconut cream or milk
½ avocado, stone and skin removed
1 handful of silverbeet, spinach
   or kale leaves, central stems
   removed, leaves roughly chopped
1 handful of mint or flat-leaf
   parsley leaves
1 egg
8 macadamia nuts, soaked for
   2 hours then drained
¼ teaspoon ground cinnamon
1 tablespoon coconut oil or MCT oil
   (see Note page 255)
filtered water, nut milk or
   coconut milk, as needed

Generally, when it comes to how much sugar they contain, smoothies from juice bars are hardly any better than chugging down soft drinks. And even though these smoothies are made with real fruit, they will still play havoc with your blood-sugar levels. So, what is the answer if you feel like a smoothie? Well, when it comes to a meal in a glass, this delicious fat bomb smoothie is the bee's knees. Fill yourself up with this instead!

Add the coconut cream or milk, avocado, your chosen green and herb leaves, the egg, macadamias, cinnamon and oil to a blender and blend until smooth. Slowly pour in the filtered water, nut milk or coconut milk until you reach the desired consistency. Whiz again and serve immediately in tall glasses.

TIP
You can pre-soak the nuts and store them in an airtight container in the fridge for up to 4 days.

NIC'S FAMOUS WARM COCONUT CHAI

SERVES 2–4

4 cinnamon sticks

16 cardamom pods, bruised

16 cloves

5 cm piece of ginger, sliced

1 teaspoon black peppercorns

1 teaspoon fennel seeds

4 star anise

1 tablespoon tulsi tea leaves
   (caffeine-free)

3 tablespoons coconut cream
   or coconut milk, or more
   to your liking

honey or liquid stevia, to taste
   (optional)

My wonderful wife, Nic, is the queen of our kitchen, and loves whipping up healing meals and drinks for our family and guests. Her warm coconut chai is nearly as famous as her tea ceremonies. Chai, a wonderfully fragrant spiced tea that originates from India, is a very popular beverage all around the world. Traditionally made with black tea leaves, cinnamon, cardamom, ginger, black pepper and cloves, here, to add that wonderful element of fat that will keep you satiated for longer, we have used coconut cream or coconut milk as the base. I encourage you to try this as a warming drink in the cooler months or enjoy it chilled or served over ice in summer.

Bring 750 ml of water to the boil in a saucepan. Reduce the heat to low, add the spices and tea leaves and gently simmer for 15 minutes to allow the flavours to develop. Stir in the coconut cream or milk and bring to a simmer, then remove from the heat.

Strain the tea through a fine strainer into a heatproof jug or teapot and pour into mugs. Stir a little honey or stevia into the chai for a touch of sweetness, if desired.

MACADAMIA MILK

MAKES 1 LITRE

160 g (1 cup) macadamia nuts
2 litres (8 cups) filtered water

Making your own nut milk is pretty simple; however, it can be a little expensive if you are going to be having a lot of it. And, to be honest, having too many nuts isn't advisable, as they are high in omega-6 fatty acids, which we are trying to reduce in our diets. I tend to eat no more than a handful of nuts a week. Make sure you only ever use organic raw nuts and if you are replacing your dairy milk, then give this simple macadamia milk recipe a whirl or try the coconut milk recipe on page 264.

You will need a 1 litre glass bottle or jar for this recipe. Wash the bottle or jar in very hot water or run it through a hot rinse cycle in the dishwasher.

Place the macadamia nuts in a bowl, cover with 1 litre of water and soak for 8 hours or overnight. Drain and rinse well.

Place the nuts and the remaining water in a high-powered blender and blend until smooth.

Place a strainer over a large bowl, then line the strainer with a piece of muslin that is large enough to hang over the edge of the strainer (alternatively, you can use a nut-milk bag). Tip in the macadamia mixture, pick up the edges of the muslin, bring them together and twist to squeeze out all the milk. (The leftover solids can be used in place of macadamia or almond meal when baking or making bliss balls.)

Pour the nut milk into the prepared bottle or jar and store in the fridge for up to 1 week. Shake the bottle before use as the milk will settle and separate over time.

COCONUT MILK

MAKES 700 ML

1 litre (4 cups) filtered water
190 g (2 cups) unsweetened
   shredded coconut (see Note)

A lot of coconut milks these days are stored in cans and have some nasties added to them, so it is always important to read the labels on everything you buy. Interestingly enough, making your own coconut milk can be super quick and easy to do if you want to give it a go. You can use the end result in everything from curries and broths to mueslis, desserts, smoothies and teas. This coconut milk is not suitable for whipping.

You will need a 750 ml glass bottle or jar for this recipe. Wash the bottle or jar in very hot water or run it through a hot rinse cycle in the dishwasher.

Pour the water into a saucepan, place over medium heat and bring to a simmer. Remove from the heat.

Place the coconut in a blender and add the hot water. Stir with a spoon, then allow to cool to warm. Carefully blend or pulse on high for 2–5 minutes until the milk is thick and creamy.

Strain the milk through a colander lined with two layers of muslin into a bowl. Pick up the edges of the muslin, bring them together and twist to squeeze out the remaining milk. Pour the milk into the prepared bottle or jar and store in the fridge for up to 3–4 days. Shake well before use as the milk will settle and separate over time.

NOTE
Try to source organic shredded coconut, as non-organic products can contain a lot of sulphites.

WONDER TONIC

MAKES 700 ML

800 ml apple cider vinegar,
plus extra if needed

2 long red chillies, cut in half
lengthways

5 cm piece of fresh turmeric,
thinly sliced

2.5 cm piece of ginger, thinly sliced

5 cm piece of fresh horseradish,
thinly sliced

2 garlic cloves, thinly sliced

½ onion, sliced

1 teaspoon yellow mustard seeds

½ celery stalk, sliced

⅓ carrot, sliced

¼ orange, sliced

¼ lemon, sliced

1 rosemary sprig

2 oregano sprigs

2 thyme sprigs

1 flat-leaf parsley stalk

1 bay leaf

1 teaspoon black peppercorns

1 teaspoon sea salt

1 tablespoon honey

I first tried this flavoursome tonic about seven years ago at a farmers' market in Portland, Oregon, and instantly fell in love with it. Now I have a teaspoon or two most days. It is very simple and enjoyable to make – and it looks awesome on your kitchen bench. Flavouring the apple cider vinegar with medicinal spices and herbs turns this from a mere drink into a wonder tonic that is said to have curative properties. It is certainly a great pick-me-up that has become part of my lifestyle.

You will need a 1.5 litre preserving jar with an airlock lid for this recipe. Wash the jar and utensils thoroughly in very hot soapy water, then run them through the dishwasher on a hot rinse cycle to sterilise. Alternatively, place them in a large saucepan filled with water and boil for 10 minutes. Place on a baking tray in a 150°C oven to dry.

Combine all the ingredients except the honey in a glass or stainless steel bowl and mix well.

Fill the sterilised jar with the vegetable, herb and spice mixture, pressing down well with a large spoon or potato masher to remove any air pockets. The vegetables, herbs and spices should be completely submerged in the liquid, so add more vinegar if necessary. Close the lid, then wrap a tea towel around the jar to block out the light.

Store the jar in a dark place with a temperature of 16–23°C for 6–8 weeks. (You can place the jar in an esky to maintain a more consistent temperature.) Shake the jar every day for the first week, then once every week until it's ready.

Strain the tonic into a clean jar with a lid. Discard the vegetables, herbs and spices. Stir through the honey. Store in a cool, dark place in the pantry for up to 12 months.

HELEN'S TONIC TEA

SERVES 4

2 tablespoons licorice root sticks*
1 teaspoon marshmallow root*
500 ml (2 cups) boiling
   filtered water
500 ml (2 cups) cold filtered water
½ teaspoon chia seeds
1 teaspoon ground cinnamon
½ teaspoon slippery elm powder*
2 teaspoons lemon juice,
   plus extra if needed
ice cubes (optional)

* See Glossary

This satisfying, silky and somewhat sweet tea is wonderfully soothing for the lining of your gut. Licorice, marshmallow root, chia seeds and slippery elm have anti-inflammatory properties, while lemon helps to improve water absorption, stimulate the liver and improve digestion. The gentle sweetness of licorice and cinnamon can help put any sweet cravings at bay, as well as help regulate insulin levels while you adjust to a low-carb diet.

Place the licorice and marshmallow root in a teapot or jug and pour in the boiling water. Allow to steep and cool for 15 minutes.

While the tea is steeping, place the cold water, chia seeds, cinnamon, slippery elm and lemon juice in a blender. Blend on high speed until smooth. Pour through a fine strainer into a jug.

Strain the steeped tea into the chia and cinnamon mixture. Stir, taste and add more lemon juice if needed. Chill the tea before drinking, or serve over ice, if you prefer. You can also drink it warm.

7

FATS

OLIVE OIL ICE CUBES WITH CHILLI, GARLIC AND HERBS

MAKES ABOUT 20 CUBES

1 handful of flat-leaf parsley or
   coriander leaves or a mixture
   of both
3–4 garlic cloves, finely chopped
1–2 long red chillies, sliced
   (optional)
extra-virgin olive oil,
   to fill ice-cube trays

This is a fun way to make flavoured fat ice cubes, so that when you want to add some punch to your vegetables or cooked steak or fish, you can simply pop a cube out to defrost for 20 minutes for an instant flavour hit. This cuts down so much time in the kitchen, letting you quickly and easily get some good-quality fats into your diet without the effort of peeling and cutting garlic and herbs each time you want to flavour your meal.

Roughly chop the herbs and divide evenly between the cavities in two ice-cube trays. Top with the garlic and chilli (at this stage the cavities will be half full). Pour on enough olive oil to completely fill each cavity. Cover with plastic wrap or a fitted lid and place in the freezer for 8 hours or more.

To store, you can leave the ice cubes in the trays and pop them out when ready to use or transfer them to a container and store them in the freezer for up to 3 months.

TIP
Feel free to play around with the herbs you use. You can try thyme, rosemary, sage, tarragon, mint, dill, etc.

TURMERIC AND TALLOW BUTTER

MAKES 440 G

400 g tallow, at room temperature
½ teaspoon ground turmeric
1 tablespoon olive oil
2 tablespoons coconut cream
sea salt

This amazing turmeric- and garlic-flavoured tallow 'butter' is one of my favourite things to slather over vegetables, meat, fish or seed bread. You can use this for cooking your veggies, meat and seafood in, too, as well as for making hollandaise sauce.

Place the tallow, turmeric, olive oil and coconut cream in a food processor and blend until smooth and creamy. Season with salt. Store in an airtight container in the fridge for up to 1 week.

RENDERED ANIMAL FAT

MAKES UP TO 600 G

1 kg pork back fat, beef fat, lamb fat,
    duck skin or chicken skin
    (see Note)
125 ml (½ cup) filtered water

Rendering animal fat is one of the oldest forms of cooking, and once you have the fat, it is actually one of the healthiest forms of dietary fat to consume. This is how, generations ago, our great-grandparents and their ancestors made fat for use in their own homes. I hope to see this making a resurgence in the coming years and becoming something that parents can teach their children. Luckily, many local butchers and health-food stores are now selling these kinds of fats again, so you can purchase some that is ready to go if that's easier for you.

If using pork, beef or lamb fat, trim any flesh from the fat with a sharp knife and cut the fat into 2 cm dice.

Place the fat or skin and water in a large heavy-based saucepan over low heat and simmer, stirring occasionally (taking care as the fat may spit), for 3½–4 hours until the water has evaporated and the fat is golden brown and liquefied. Try and keep the fat at around 100°C (use a candy thermometer to test the temperature). You will notice little solid bits of brown crackling floating to the surface and a lot of clear liquid; this is an indication that the fat has rendered and is ready to be taken off the heat.

Allow the rendered fat to cool a little before straining through a fine sieve into a jug, jars, containers or ice-cube trays. Save the leftover crackling bits as they make a delicious snack. The cooled melted fat will be creamy white in colour. Store, covered, in the fridge for up to 3 months or freeze for up to 9 months.

NOTE
You can buy pork, beef and lamb fat or duck and chicken skin from your local butcher. They may need to be ordered in advance.

TIP
You can also use a slow cooker,
as it maintains a gentle heat and
works perfectly for rendering fat.

8

BASICS

AIOLI

MAKES ABOUT 400 G

6 garlic confit cloves (page 288)
2 egg yolks
1 teaspoon Dijon mustard
1 tablespoon apple cider vinegar
juice of ½ lemon
310 ml (1 ¼ cups) olive oil,
    plus extra if needed
sea salt and freshly ground
    black pepper

Combine the garlic, egg yolks, mustard, vinegar, lemon juice and oil in a glass jug or jar. Using a hand-held blender, blend, working the blade from the bottom of the jug slowly to the top, until thick and creamy. Alternatively, place the garlic, egg yolks, mustard, vinegar and lemon juice in the bowl of a food processor and process until combined. With the motor running, slowly pour in the oil in a thin, steady stream and process until the aioli is thick and creamy. Add extra olive oil if the aioli is too thick. Season with salt and pepper. Store in an airtight container in the fridge for 4–5 days.

BÉARNAISE SAUCE >

MAKES 300 G

150 ml white wine (such as
    chardonnay)
3 tablespoons white wine vinegar
    or apple cider vinegar
2 French shallots, finely chopped
1 teaspoon black peppercorns
1 bay leaf
250 ml (1 cup) coconut oil
3 egg yolks
1 tablespoon chopped tarragon
    leaves
sea salt and freshly ground
    white pepper

Place the white wine, vinegar, shallot, peppercorns and bay leaf in a saucepan. Bring to the boil and simmer for 5–8 minutes until the liquid is reduced to 2 tablespoons. Strain through a fine sieve into the jug of a blender. Discard the shallot, peppercorns and bay leaf.

Melt the coconut oil in a saucepan until hot (45–48°C).

Add the egg yolks to the vinegar mixture in the blender. With the blender on low, slowly pour in the hot coconut oil in a thin, steady stream and blend until thickened. Transfer to a bowl, fold in the tarragon and season with salt and pepper. Serve immediately over steak, fish or your favourite vegetables.

BEEF BONE BROTH

MAKES 3.5–4 LITRES

about 2 kg beef knuckle and
    marrow bones
1 calf foot, chopped into pieces
    (optional)
3 tablespoons apple cider vinegar
1.5 kg meaty beef rib or neck bones
3 onions, roughly chopped
3 carrots, roughly chopped
3 celery stalks, roughly chopped
2 leeks, white part only,
    roughly chopped
3 thyme sprigs
2 bay leaves
1 teaspoon black peppercorns,
    crushed
1 garlic bulb, cut in half horizontally
2 large handfuls of flat-leaf
    parsley stalks

Place the knuckle and marrow bones and calf foot (if using) in a stockpot, add the vinegar and pour in 5 litres of cold water, or enough to cover. Set aside for 1 hour to help draw out the nutrients from the bones. Remove the bones from the water, reserving the water.

Preheat the oven to 180°C.

Place the knuckle and marrow bones, calf foot (if using) and meaty bones in a few large roasting tins and roast in the oven for 30–40 minutes until well browned. Return all the bones to the pot and add the vegetables.

Pour the fat from the roasting tins into a saucepan, add 1 litre of the reserved water, place over high heat and bring to a simmer, stirring with a wooden spoon to loosen any coagulated juices. Add this liquid to the bones and vegetables. If necessary, add the remaining reserved water to the pot to just cover the bones – the liquid should come no higher than 2 cm below the rim of the pot, as the volume will increase slightly during cooking.

Bring the broth to the boil, skimming off the scum that rises to the top. Reduce the heat to low and add the thyme, bay leaves, peppercorns and garlic. Simmer for 12–24 hours. Just before finishing, add the parsley and simmer for 10 minutes. Strain the broth into a large container, cover and place in the fridge overnight. Remove the congealed fat that rises to the top and reserve for cooking; it will keep in the fridge for up to 1 week or in the freezer for up to 3 months. Transfer the thick and gelatinous broth to smaller airtight containers and place in the fridge or, for long-term storage, the freezer. The broth can be stored in the fridge for 3–4 days or frozen for up to 3 months.

BROCCOLI RICE

SERVES 4

2 heads of broccoli (about 800 g),
   roughly chopped into florets
2 tablespoons coconut oil or
   good-quality animal fat*
sea salt and freshly ground
   black pepper

* See Glossary

Place the broccoli in the bowl of a food processor and pulse into tiny, fine pieces that look like rice.

Heat the oil or fat in a large frying pan over medium heat, add the broccoli and cook, stirring occasionally, for 4–5 minutes until tender. Season with salt and pepper and serve with stews, stir-fries and curries.

CAULIFLOWER RICE

SERVES 4

1 head of cauliflower (about 1 kg),
   florets and stems roughly
   chopped
2 tablespoons coconut oil or
   good-quality animal fat*
sea salt and freshly ground
   black pepper

* See Glossary

Place the cauliflower in the bowl of a food processor and pulse into tiny, fine pieces that look like rice.

Melt the coconut oil or fat in a large frying pan over medium heat. Add the cauliflower and cook for 4–6 minutes until softened. Season with salt and pepper and serve.

CHICKEN BONE BROTH

MAKES 3.5 LITRES

1–1.5 kg bony chicken parts
    (I like to use necks, backs,
    breastbones and wings)
2–4 chicken feet (optional)
2 tablespoons apple cider vinegar
1 large onion, roughly chopped
2 carrots, roughly chopped
3 celery stalks, roughly chopped
2 leeks, white part only,
    roughly chopped
1 garlic bulb, cut in half horizontally
1 tablespoon black peppercorns,
    lightly crushed
2 bay leaves
2 large handfuls of flat-leaf
    parsley stalks

Place the chicken pieces in a stockpot, add 5 litres of cold water and the remaining ingredients and let stand for 1 hour to help draw out the nutrients from the bones.

Place the pot over medium–high heat and bring to the boil, skimming off the scum that forms on the surface of the liquid. Reduce the heat to low and simmer for 12–24 hours. The longer you cook the broth, the richer and more flavourful it will be.

Strain the broth through a fine sieve into a large storage container, cover and place in the fridge overnight until the fat rises to the top and congeals. Skim off the fat and reserve for cooking; it will keep in the fridge for up to 1 week or in the freezer for up to 3 months. Transfer the broth to smaller airtight containers and place in the fridge or, for long-term storage, the freezer. The broth can be stored in the fridge for 3–4 days or frozen for up to 3 months.

NOTE

To make chicken bone broth using a pressure cooker, use only enough cold water to just cover the meat and vegetables. (Your cooker should be no more than two-thirds full, otherwise hot liquid may spray out.) Close the lid and lock it, then bring the cooker to high pressure and cook over medium–low heat for 2 hours. Let the pressure drop naturally before opening the lid. If using a slow cooker, add only enough cold water to just cover. Cover with the lid and cook on low for 12 hours.

CHILLI OIL

MAKES 400 ML

400 ml olive oil
4 tablespoons chilli flakes

Gently warm the olive oil in a saucepan over low heat. Add the chilli flakes and warm through for 2 minutes. Do not boil. Remove from the heat and set aside to cool. Store in a resealable glass bottle in a cool, dark place. Shake the bottle every week or so. The longer you leave it, the hotter and redder the oil becomes.

COCONUT FLOUR PITA BREAD

MAKES 8

3 tablespoons coconut flour
3 tablespoons arrowroot*
2 tablespoons almond meal
½ teaspoon fine sea salt
8 large egg whites
2 tablespoons coconut oil

* See Glossary

Whisk the coconut flour, arrowroot, almond meal, salt, egg whites and 125 ml of water in a large bowl to make a smooth batter.

Melt 1 teaspoon of oil in a small frying pan over medium–high heat. Pour about 3 tablespoons of batter into the pan. Slightly tilt the pan to swirl the batter and spread it out to form a thin round, about 13 cm in diameter. Cook for 2 minutes until golden brown, then flip and cook the other side until lightly golden. Transfer the pita bread to a plate and keep warm. Repeat until you have used all the batter. Store in a container or zip-lock bag in the fridge for up to 1 week or freeze for up to 3 months.

DASHI BROTH

MAKES 1.4 LITRES

3 sheets dried kombu*
   (each 11 cm × 15 cm)
50 g (2 heaped cups) bonito flakes*
1 teaspoon sea salt
1 ½ teaspoons tamari or
   coconut aminos*

* See Glossary

Cut small slits in the kombu with a pair of scissors or tear with your hands to help release the flavour. Place the kombu and 1.5 litres of water in a large saucepan and set aside to soak for about 1 hour until the kombu starts to soften.

Place the pan over medium–low heat and bring to a gentle simmer (ideally 60–71°C), making sure that the water does not boil. (Boiling the kombu gives the dashi an intense flavour and turns the broth cloudy. Cooking the kombu at a lower temperature yields a clearer broth.) Cook gently for 1 hour until the kombu is tender enough to be pierced easily with a chopstick and the broth has a mild sea-like aroma and a noticeable but delicate salty flavour. Strain the broth, discarding the kombu.

Return the broth to the pan and warm over medium–low heat until steam rises from the surface of the liquid (about 85°C). Add the bonito flakes and salt and push down gently with a spoon to submerge the flakes; you do not want to break up the fine pieces. Turn off the heat and let the bonito flakes steep in the hot broth for 5 minutes.

Strain the dashi broth through a fine sieve into a jug, taking care not to squeeze or press the flakes. Discard the bonito flakes.

Season the dashi with the tamari or coconut aminos. If not using immediately, let the dashi cool at room temperature until lukewarm, about 30 minutes, then refrigerate, uncovered, until completely cool. Cover and refrigerate for up to 3 days or freeze for up to 3 months.

FERMENTED AIOLI

MAKES 550 G

150 g Sauerkraut (page 295),
   plus 1 tablespoon sauerkraut juice
400 g Aioli (page 280)
sea salt and freshly ground
   black pepper

Place the sauerkraut in a blender or food processor and blend until smooth, then mix through the sauerkraut juice and aioli. Season with salt and pepper, if needed. Store in an airtight container in the fridge for 4–5 days.

FERMENTED KIMCHI MAYONNAISE

MAKES 550 G

150 g Kimchi (page 290),
   plus 1 tablespoon kimchi juice
400 g Mayonnaise (page 292)
sea salt and freshly ground
   black pepper (optional)

Place the kimchi in a blender or food processor and blend until smooth. Mix through the kimchi juice and mayonnaise. Season with salt and pepper, if needed. Store in a glass jar or airtight container in the fridge for up to 1 week.

FISH BONE BROTH

MAKES 3 LITRES

2 tablespoons coconut oil
2 celery stalks, roughly chopped
2 onions, roughly chopped
1 carrot, roughly chopped
125 ml (½ cup) dry white wine
   or vermouth (optional)
3 or 4 whole, non-oily fish carcasses
   (including heads), such as
   snapper, barramundi or kingfish
3 tablespoons apple cider vinegar
1 handful of thyme and flat-leaf
   parsley sprigs
1 bay leaf

Melt the oil in a stockpot or large saucepan over medium–low heat. Add the vegetables and cook gently for 30–60 minutes until soft. Pour in the wine or vermouth (if using) and bring to the boil. Add the fish carcasses and cover with 3.5 litres of cold water. Stir in the vinegar and bring to the boil, skimming off the scum and any impurities as they rise to the top.

Tie the herbs together with kitchen string and add to the saucepan. Reduce the heat to low, cover and simmer for at least 3 hours.

Remove the fish carcasses with tongs or a slotted spoon and strain the liquid through a sieve into a large storage container. Cover and place in the fridge overnight so that the fat rises to the top and congeals. Remove the fat and reserve it for cooking; it will keep in the fridge for up to 1 week or in the freezer for up to 3 months. Transfer the broth to smaller airtight containers. The broth should be thick and gelatinous – the longer you cook the bones for, the more gelatinous it will become. Store in the fridge for 3–4 days or in the freezer for up to 3 months.

GARLIC OIL

MAKES 250 ML (1 CUP)

40 garlic cloves, peeled
250 ml (1 cup) olive oil

Place the garlic and oil in a small saucepan over very low heat (you don't want the oil to boil). Cook for 1 hour until the garlic is very soft. Store the garlic and oil in a sterilised resealable jar in the fridge for up to 3 months. The creamy, soft garlic confit cloves can be used in aioli (page 280).

GREEN GODDESS DRESSING

MAKES 250 ML (1 CUP)

½ avocado
3 tablespoons coconut milk
3 tablespoons lemon juice
1 garlic clove, finely chopped
2 anchovy fillets, finely chopped
2 large handfuls of chopped
   flat-leaf parsley leaves
3 tablespoons chopped basil leaves
1 tablespoon chopped tarragon
   leaves
¼ teaspoon salt
125 ml (½ cup) extra-virgin olive oil

Place the avocado, coconut milk, lemon juice, garlic, anchovies, herbs and salt in the bowl of a food processor and process until well combined. With the motor running, slowly pour in the oil and process until the dressing thickens and the herbs are finely chopped. Store in a glass jar in the fridge for up to 5 days.

HOLLANDAISE SAUCE

MAKES 150 G

120 ml coconut oil
4 egg yolks
2 tablespoons lemon juice
or apple cider vinegar
½ teaspoon sea salt
2 pinches of sweet paprika
(optional)

Melt the coconut oil in a saucepan to 50°C or until hot.

Combine the egg yolks and lemon juice or vinegar in a blender. With the blender on low, slowly pour in the hot coconut oil in a thin, steady stream. Season with salt and paprika (if using), then pulse a few times to thicken. Serve immediately with poached eggs or your favourite vegetables.

JUS

MAKES 400 ML

2 tablespoons coconut oil or
duck fat, melted
100 g French shallots, sliced
1 garlic clove, lightly crushed
4 thyme sprigs
1 tablespoon tomato paste
200 ml red wine (such as shiraz)
1.25 litres Chicken or Beef Bone
Broth (pages 284 and 282)
sea salt and freshly ground
black pepper

Melt 1 tablespoon of oil or fat in a saucepan over medium–high heat. Add the shallot and sauté, stirring occasionally, for 5 minutes until lightly caramelised. Add the garlic, thyme and tomato paste and continue to cook for 3 minutes. Pour in the wine, bring to the boil and simmer until reduced by two-thirds. Pour in the broth and bring to the boil. Turn the heat down to medium and simmer, occasionally skimming the scum that rises to the surface, until the jus is reduced by two-thirds and has a sauce-like consistency.

Strain through a sieve, season with salt and pepper and serve.

KIMCHI

MAKES 1 × 1.5 LITRE JAR

½ Chinese cabbage (wong bok)
   (about 500 g)
3 radishes or 1 daikon
1 carrot
1 onion
1 ½ teaspoons sea salt
3–4 garlic cloves, thinly sliced
3 tablespoons grated ginger
3–4 long red chillies, deseeded
   and thinly sliced
2 large handfuls of coriander roots,
   stalks and leaves, finely chopped
1 tablespoon Korean chilli powder
   (gochugaru)* (optional)
1 teaspoon ground turmeric
   (optional)
1 sachet vegetable starter culture*
   (this will weigh 2–5 g,
   depending on the brand)

* See Glossary

You will need a 1.5 litre preserving jar with an airlock lid for this recipe. Wash the jar and utensils thoroughly in very hot water or run them through a hot rinse cycle in the dishwasher.

Remove the outer leaves of the cabbage. Choose an unblemished leaf, wash it well and set aside. Finely shred the remaining cabbage, radishes or daikon, carrot and onion in a food processor. (You can also use a mandoline or knife to chop them finely.) In a large glass or stainless steel bowl, combine the cabbage with the radish or daikon, carrot and onion. Sprinkle on the salt and mix well. Add the garlic, ginger, chilli, coriander, chilli powder and turmeric (if using). Mix well, cover and set aside.

Dissolve the starter culture in water according to the packet instructions (the amount of water will depend on the brand). Add to the vegetables and mix well. Fill the prepared jar with the vegetable mix, pressing down well with a large spoon or a potato masher to remove any air pockets. Leave 2 cm of room free at the top. The vegetables should be completely submerged in the liquid, so add more water if necessary.

Fold up the clean reserved cabbage leaf, place it on top of the mixture and add a small glass weight (a shot glass is ideal) to keep everything submerged. Close the lid, then wrap a tea towel around the jar to block out the light. Store in a dark place at 16–23°C for 10–14 days. (You can place the jar in an esky to maintain a more consistent temperature.) Different vegetables have different culturing times and the warmer it is, the shorter the time needed. The longer you leave the jar, the higher the level of good bacteria present and the tangier the flavour.

Chill the kimchi before eating. Once opened, it will last for up to 2 months in the fridge when kept submerged in the liquid. If unopened, it will keep for up to 9 months in the fridge.

KRAUT DRESSING

MAKES 300 ML

100 ml sauerkraut brine (page 295)
200 ml avocado oil or
    extra-virgin olive oil
finely grated zest of 1 lemon
8 lemon balm leaves, torn (see Note)
3 cardamom pods, crushed
¼ teaspoon ground cumin
pinch of sea salt and freshly ground
    black pepper

Combine all the ingredients in a small bowl and mix well. Leave to stand at room temperature for a few hours to allow the flavours to develop.

Drizzle the dressing over your favourite salad or steamed veggies. Store leftovers in a sealed jar in the fridge for up to 1 week.

NOTE

If you are having trouble finding lemon balm, feel free to use mint leaves instead.

MAYONNAISE

MAKES ABOUT 500 G

4 egg yolks
1 ½ tablespoons Dijon mustard
1 ½ tablespoons apple cider vinegar
1 tablespoon lemon juice
400 ml olive oil or macadamia oil,
   or 200 ml of each
sea salt and freshly ground
   black pepper

1 Place the egg yolks, mustard, vinegar, lemon juice, oil and a pinch of salt in a glass jug or jar.

2 Blend with a hand-held blender until smooth and creamy, working the blade from the bottom of the jug very slowly up to the top.

3 Season with salt and pepper.

4 Store in a sealed glass jar in the fridge for 4–5 days.

TIP
Alternatively, you can place the egg yolks, mustard, vinegar, lemon juice and a pinch of salt in the bowl of a food processor and process until combined. With the motor running, slowly pour in the oil in a thin, steady stream and process until the mayonnaise is thick and creamy. Season with salt and pepper and store as above.

STEP 1

STEP 2

STEP 3

STEP 4

NUT MUESLI

MAKES 300 G

40 g (¼ cup) cashew nuts (activated
   if possible*), roughly chopped
40 g (¼ cup) macadamia nuts
   (activated if possible*),
   roughly chopped
40 g (¼ cup) almonds (activated
   if possible*), roughly chopped
25 g (¼ cup) walnuts (activated
   if possible*), roughly chopped
2 tablespoons sunflower seeds
   (activated if possible*)
2 tablespoons pumpkin seeds
   (activated if possible*)
2 tablespoons flaxseeds
2 tablespoons currants
3 tablespoons coconut flakes

* See Glossary

Mix all the ingredients together to combine. Store in an airtight glass
container in the pantry for up to 4 weeks.

NUT-FREE PALEO WRAPS

MAKES 8

6 eggs
200 ml coconut milk
2 tablespoons coconut oil, melted
3 tablespoons coconut flour
3 tablespoons tapioca flour*
½ teaspoon sea salt

* See Glossary

Place the eggs, coconut milk, 1 tablespoon of coconut oil and
1 tablespoon of water in a bowl and whisk until smooth. Add the
dry ingredients and whisk well to combine. To allow the dry
ingredients to absorb the liquid, stand for 5–10 minutes. The batter
is ready when it coats the back of a spoon.

Melt 1 teaspoon of the remaining oil in a small frying pan over
medium–high heat. Give the batter a good mix, then pour about
80 ml (⅓ cup) of batter into the pan. Slightly tilt and swirl the
pan to spread the batter over the base and form a round about
20 cm in diameter. Cook for 1–2 minutes, or until golden brown
on the underside. Flip and cook on the other side for about
30 seconds until lightly golden. Transfer to a plate and keep warm.
Repeat until you have eight wraps.

Wrap leftovers in plastic wrap and store in the fridge or freezer.

SAUERKRAUT

MAKES 1 × 1.5 LITRE JAR

400 g green cabbage
400 g red cabbage
1 beetroot, peeled
2 carrots (about 250 g in total)
1 ½ teaspoons sea salt
1 sachet vegetable starter culture*
    (this will weigh 2–5 g, depending
    on the brand)

* See Glossary

You will need a 1.5 litre preserving jar with an airlock lid for this recipe. Wash the jar and utensils thoroughly in very hot water. Alternatively, run them through a hot rinse cycle in the dishwasher.

Remove the outer leaves of the cabbages. Choose an unblemished leaf, wash it well and set aside.

Shred the cabbages, beetroot and carrot in a food processor or slice with a knife or mandoline, then transfer to a large glass or stainless steel bowl. Sprinkle the salt over the vegetables, mix well and cover with a plate.

Prepare the starter culture according to the directions on the packet. Add to the vegetables and mix thoroughly.

Using a large spoon, fill the prepared jar with the vegetable mixture, pressing down well to remove any air pockets and leaving 2 cm free at the top. The vegetables should be completely submerged in the liquid. Add more water, if necessary.

Take the clean reserved cabbage leaf, fold it up and place it on top of the vegetables, then add a small glass weight (a shot glass is ideal) to keep everything submerged. Close the lid and wrap a tea towel around the jar to block out the light. Store in a dark place at 16–23°C for 10–14 days. (You can place the jar in an esky to maintain a more consistent temperature.) Different vegetables have different culturing times and the warmer it is, the shorter the time needed. The longer you leave the jar, the higher the level of good bacteria present. It is up to you how long you leave it – some people prefer the tangier flavour that comes with extra fermenting time, while others prefer a milder flavour.

Chill before eating. Once opened, it will last for up to 2 months in the fridge when kept submerged in liquid. If unopened, it will keep for up to 9 months in the fridge. Don't throw out the brine – it can be used for a delicious dressing like the one on page 291.

SRIRACHA CHILLI SAUCE

MAKES 625 G

680 g long red chillies, deseeded
    and roughly chopped
8 garlic cloves, crushed
80 ml (⅓ cup) apple cider vinegar
3 tablespoons tomato paste
1 large medjool date, pitted
2 tablespoons fish sauce
1 ½ teaspoons sea salt
2 tablespoons extra-virgin olive oil

Combine all the ingredients with 80 ml (⅓ cup) of water in the bowl of a food processor and process until smooth. Pour into a saucepan and, stirring occasionally, bring to the boil over high heat. Reduce the heat to low and simmer, stirring now and then, for 5–10 minutes until the sauce is vibrant and red. Remove from the heat and cool. Once cool, add the olive oil and use a hand-held blender to blend until smooth. Transfer to a large airtight glass jar and store in the fridge for up to 2 weeks.

TOMATO KETCHUP

MAKES ABOUT 300 ML

180 g tomato paste
1 tablespoon apple cider vinegar
1 teaspoon garlic powder
1 teaspoon onion powder
1 teaspoon ground cinnamon
¼ teaspoon freshly grated nutmeg
⅛ teaspoon ground cloves
1 teaspoon honey (optional)

Combine the tomato paste and 80 ml (⅓ cup) of water in a small saucepan over medium heat and bring to a simmer. Remove from the heat and stir in the remaining ingredients until fully incorporated. (Stir in more water if you'd prefer a thinner sauce.)

Allow the sauce to cool, then pour into a glass jar or container, cover and store in the fridge for 2–4 weeks.

WORCESTERSHIRE SAUCE

MAKES 125 ML (½ CUP)

125 ml (½ cup) apple cider vinegar
2 ½ tablespoons tamari or
    coconut aminos*
½ teaspoon ground ginger
½ teaspoon mustard powder
½ teaspoon onion powder
½ teaspoon garlic powder
¼ teaspoon ground cinnamon
¼ teaspoon freshly ground
    black pepper
2 tablespoons filtered water

* See Glossary

Combine all the ingredients in a saucepan and, stirring occasionally, bring to the boil over medium heat. Turn down the heat to low and simmer for 10 minutes. Remove from the heat and allow to cool. Pour into a sterilised bottle and store in the fridge for up to 1 month.

GLOSSARY

Activated seeds and nuts

Nuts and seeds are a great source of healthy fats, but they contain phytic acid, which binds to minerals such as iron, zinc, calcium, potassium and magnesium so that they can't be readily absorbed. Activating nuts and seeds lessens the phytates, so we absorb as many of the good things as possible. Activated nuts and seeds are available from health-food stores. Or to save money and make your own, simply soak the nuts in filtered water (hard nuts, such as almonds, need to soak for 12 hours; softer nuts, such as cashews and macadamias, only need 4–6 hours). Rinse the nuts under running water, then spread out on a baking tray and place in a 50°C oven or dehydrator to dry out. This will take anywhere from 6 to 24 hours, depending on the temperature and the kind of nuts or seeds. Store in an airtight container in the pantry for up to 3 months.

Arrowroot

Arrowroot is a starch made from the roots of several tropical plants. In Australia, arrowroot and tapioca flour are considered the same, even though they are actually from different plants. It can be found at health-food stores and some supermarkets. *See also* Tapioca flour.

Baharat

Baharat is a Middle Eastern spice blend that usually includes black pepper, coriander, paprika, cardamon, nutmeg, cumin, cloves and cinnamon. Baharat is great for seasoning meats and vegetables, adding to dips and sauces, or using as a dry rub for marinade or veggies, meat and fish. Look for baharat at Middle Eastern grocers or delis.

Bonito flakes

Bonito flakes are made from the bonito fish, which is like a small tuna. The fish is smoked, fermented, dried and shaved, and the end product looks similar to wood shavings. Bonito flakes are used to garnish Japanese dishes, to make sauces such as ponzu and soups such as miso, and to make the Japanese stock dashi. You can find bonito flakes in Asian food stores.

Coconut aminos

Made from coconut sap, coconut aminos is similar in flavour to a light soy sauce. Because it is free of both soy and gluten, it makes a great paleo alternative to soy sauce and tamari. Coconut aminos is available at health-food stores.

Coconut oil

Coconut oil is extracted from the meat of mature coconuts. It has a high smoke point, making it great for cooking at high temperatures. The viscosity of coconut oil changes depending on the temperature and ranges from liquid to solid. Although coconut oil is high in saturated fats, they are mainly medium-chain saturated fatty acids, which means the body can use them quickly and does not have to store them. Coconut oil is available from supermarkets and health-food stores. Look for virgin cold-pressed varieties, as these have had the least amount of processing.

Good-quality animal fat

I use either coconut oil or good-quality animal fats for cooking as they have high smoke points (meaning they do not oxidise at high temperatures). Some of my favourite animal fats to use are lard (pork fat), tallow (rendered beef fat), rendered chicken fat and duck fat. These may be hard to find – ask at your local butcher or meat supplier, look online for meat suppliers who sell them or make your own when making bone broths.

Gubinge

Gubinge, also known as Kakadu plum and billygoat plum, is the world's highest natural source of vitamin C. An Australian native from the Kakadu and Kimberley regions, gubinge has been an important food source and medicine for indigenous Australians for more than 40,000 years. These small, tart fruits are rich in antioxidants, iron and vitamin E and have known antifungal, antibacterial and antiviral properties. While the fruit can be used in jams and desserts, it's most commonly available as a powder, which can be mixed into water and smoothies or sprinkled over your breakfast cereal. To retain the nutrient level, the powder is best used in cold recipes. Gubinge powder can be found online and in some health-food stores.

Kombu

Kombu is a high-protein sea vegetable, rich in calcium, iron, iodine and dietary fibre. It is salty and savoury and plays a vital role in Japanese cuisine. Kombu can be used in a similar way to bay leaves – add them to a stew or curry for a flavour boost and remove them after cooking. Kombu can be found in Asian grocers and is mainly sold dried or pickled in vinegar. Dried kombu is often covered with a white powder from natural salts and starch. It is harmless but can easily be removed with a damp cloth.

Korean chilli powder (gochugaru)

Korean chilli powder is made from thin red chillies that are dried in the sun and ground. It has smoky, fruity sweet notes, with a hot kick, and is used to make classic Korean dishes such as kimchi and bulgogi. It is also great for stir-fries, dipping sauces and meat marinades. You can find Korean chilli powder in Asian supermarkets.

Licorice root

Licorice root has been used in Chinese medicine for many years and is believed to help with a wide range of conditions, including digestive problems. When ground into a powder, licorice root has a slightly sweet flavour and can be added to smoothies, drinks and desserts. You can find it in health-food stores and online.

Marshmallow root

The marshmallow plant is a type of herb originating from Africa and has been used medicinally for centuries. It is used to relieve sore throats and dry coughs, and research suggests it can help treat digestive issues, such as leaky gut syndrome and stomach ulcers. The leaves and roots are also used as flavouring agents in food. Marshmallow root can be found in health-food stores and online.

Nori sheets

Nori is a dark green, paper-like, toasted seaweed used in Japanese dishes. Nori provides an abundance of essential nutrients and is rich in vitamins, iron and other minerals, amino acids, omega-3 and omega-6, and antioxidants. Nori sheets are commonly used to roll sushi, but they can also be added to salads, soups and many other dishes. You can buy nori sheets from Asian grocers and most supermarkets.

Probiotic capsules

Probiotic capsules contain live bacteria that can help to regulate digestion, clear up yeast infections and assist with conditions such as irritable bowel syndrome. These capsules need to be kept in the fridge. They can be swallowed whole, or opened up and used to ferment drinks such as kefir. Probiotic capsules can be found at pharmacies and health-food stores.

Shichimi togarashi

Shichimi togarashi literally means 'seven flavour chilli pepper' and is one of the most popular condiments on Japanese tables. As the name suggests, this spice mixture is made from seven ingredients; typically shichimi togarashi includes red chilli, Japanese (sansho) peppers, orange peel, black and white sesame seeds, ginger and seaweed. The chillies aside, the ingredients vary, and if you are lucky you may come across a Japanese vendor offering a custom blend.

Slippery elm powder

Slippery elm powder comes from the inner bark of the slippery elm tree. It is believed to help the digestive system and some people also take slippery elm to help with coughs and skin problems. Slippery elm doesn't have a particularly strong flavour, so it can be added to smoothies, juices or sauces. You can buy it from heath-food stores and pharmacies.

Tapioca flour

Tapioca flour is made by grinding up the dried root of the manioc (also known as cassava) plant. It can be used to thicken dishes or in gluten-free baking. You can find tapioca flour at health-food stores and some supermarkets. *See also* Arrowroot.

Vegetable starter culture

A vegetable starter culture is a preparation used to kickstart the fermentation process when culturing vegetables and yoghurts. I use a broad-spectrum starter sourced from organic vegetables rather than one grown from dairy sources, as this ensures the highest number of living, active bacteria and produces consistently successful results free of pathogens. Vegetable starter culture usually comes in sachets and can be purchased at health-food stores or online. You can also get fresh, non-dairy starter cultures for yoghurt and kefir (we recommend kulturedwellness.com).

Wakame

Wakame is an edible seaweed used in Japanese, Korean and Chinese cuisine. It's great in soups, salads and stir-fries. Wakame contains iron, magnesium, iodine, calcium and lignans. You can find it in Asian grocers and some supermarkets.

Young coconuts

Young coconuts are harvested at around 5–7 months and are usually white in colour. To open one, cut a circle in the top using a large knife and then prise this circle off. There is usually around 250 ml (1 cup) of coconut water inside. You can then scoop out the soft flesh using a spoon. Look for young coconuts at Asian food stores, health-food stores and supermarkets.

Yuzu juice

Yuzu is a Japanese citrus fruit that has an extraordinary spicy citrus flavour, somewhere between a lemon and a lime. Yuzu juice is very high in vitamin C and is great in cocktails, dressings, dips and sashimi dishes. You can buy yuzu juice from Asian grocers.

FURTHER READING

Introduction

Adam-Perrot, A., et al. (2006). Low-carbohydrate diets: nutritional and physiological aspects. *Obesity Reviews*, 7(1), pp.49–58.

Westman, E. C. (2007). Low-carbohydrate nutrition and metabolism. *American Journal of Clinical Nutrition*, 86(2), pp.276–84.

Macronutrients: the big picture

Eenfeldt, A. (2017). A low-carb diet for beginners. Diet Doctor, May, www.dietdoctor.com/low-carb

Glucose and insulin: what you need to know

Australian Institute of Health and Welfare (2014). How Healthy Are We? Australia's Health 2014. www.aihw.gov.au/australias-health/2014/how-healthy

Salvetti, A., et al. (1993). The inter-relationship between insulin resistance and hypertension. *Drugs*, 46(Suppl. 2), pp.149–59.

Leptin: why it's key

Gedgaudas, N., *Primal Body, Primal Mind: Beyond the paleo diet for total health and a longer life*, Chapter 14, 'Leptin: The lord and master of your hormonal kingdom' (Healing Arts Press, 2011).

Gedgaudas, N., *Primal Fat Burner: Live longer, slow aging, super-power your brain, and save your life with a high-fat, low-carb paleo diet*, (Atria Books, 2017).

Klok, M. D., et al. (2007). The role of leptin and ghrelin in the regulation of food intake and body weight in humans: a review. *Obesity Reviews*, 8(1), pp.21–34.

Suga, A., et al. (2000). Effects of fructose and glucose on plasma leptin, insulin, and insulin resistance in lean and VMH-lesioned obese rats. *American Journal of Physiology, Endocrinology and Metabolism*, 278(4), pp.677–83.

Trayhurn, P. (2003). Leptin – a critical body weight signal and a 'master' hormone? *Science's STKE*, 2003(169), pe7.

'Frankenfoods': processed foods and hidden sugars

Brantley, P. J., et al. (2005). Environmental and lifestyle influences on obesity. *Journal of the Louisiana State Medical Society*, 157(Spec.1), pp.S19–27.

Brymora, A. et al. (2012). Low-fructose diet lowers blood pressure and inflammation in patients with chronic kidney disease. *Nephrology Dialysis Transplantation*, 27(2), pp.608–12.

Cordain, L. (1999). Cereal grains: humanity's double-edged sword. *World Review of Nutrition and Dietetics*, 84, pp.19–73.

Gedgaudas, N., *Primal Fat Burner: Live longer, slow aging, super-power your brain, and save your life with a high-fat, low-carb paleo diet*, Chapter 3, A is for agriculture and adapting to glucose' (Atria Books, 2017).

Glushakova, O., et al. (2008). Fructose induces the inflammatory molecule ICAM-1 in endothelial cells. *Journal of the American Society of Nephrology*, 19(9), pp.1712–20.

Gross, L. S., et al. (2004). Increased consumption of refined carbohydrates and the epidemic of type 2 diabetes in the United States: an ecologic assessment. *American Journal of Clinical Nutrition*, 79(5), pp.774–79.

European Commission DG Environment. (2012). Intensive agriculture leaves lasting legacy on soil health. *Science for Environment Policy*, 291, 5 July, ec.europa.eu/environment/integration/research/newsalert/pdf/291na4_en.pdf.

Keith, L. *The Vegetarian Myth: Food, Justice and Sustainability* (Flashpoint Press, 2009).

Manzel, A., et al. (2008). Role of 'western diet' in inflammatory autoimmune diseases. *Current Allergy and Asthma Reports*, 14(1), pp.404.

Spreadbury, I. (2012). Comparison with ancestral diets suggests dense acellular carbohydrates promote an inflammatory microbiota, and may be the primary dietary cause of leptin resistance and obesity. *Diabetes, Metabolic Syndrome and Obesity: Targets and Therapy*, 5, pp.175–89.

Uribarri, J., et al. (2005). Diet-derived advanced glycation end products are major contributors to the body's age pool and induce inflammation in healthy subjects. *Annals of the New York Academy of Sciences*, 1043, pp.461–66.

Healthy fats: filling and delicious

Al-Khalifa, A., et al., Therapeutic role of low-carbohydrate ketogenic diet in diabetes. *Nutrition*, 25(11–12), pp.1177–85.

Bueno, N. B., et al. (2013). Very-low-carbohydrate ketogenic diet v. low-fat diet for long-term weight loss: a meta-analysis of randomised controlled trials. *British Journal of Nutrition*, 110(7), pp.1178–87.

Cawthorn, W. P., et al. (2014). Bone marrow adipose tissue is an endocrine organ that contributes to increased circulating adiponectin during caloric restriction. *Cell Metabolism*, 20(2), pp.368–75.

Henderson, S. (2008). Ketone bodies as a therapeutic for Alzheimer's disease. *Neurotherapeutics*, 5(3), pp.470-480.

Nugent, S., et al. (2015). Ketones and brain development: Implications for correcting deteriorating brain glucose metabolism during aging. *OCL*, 23(1) D110.

Phinney, S. D. (2004). Ketogenic diets and physical performance. *Nutrition and Metabolism* (London), 2004(1), 2.

Simopoulos, A., (2002). The importance of the ratio of omega-6/omega-3 essential fatty acids. *Biomedicine and Pharmacotherapy*, 56(8), pp.365–79.

Simopoulos, A.P. (2016). An increase in the omega-6/omega-3 fatty acid ratio increases the risk for obesity. *Nutrients*, 8(3), 128.

VanItallie, T., et al. (2005). Treatment of Parkinson disease with diet-induced hyperketonemia: A feasibility study. *Neurology*, 64(4), pp.728-730.

Why do I need to know where the animals I eat come from?

Diez-Gonzalez, F., et al. (1998). Grain feeding and the dissemination of acid-resistant *Escherichia coli* from cattle. *Science*, 281(5383), pp.1666–68.

Very good veggies: your staple ingredients

Eenfeldt, A. (2017). Low-carb vegetables – the best and the worst. Diet Doctor, May, www.dietdoctor.com/low-carb/vegetables

Nicastro, H. L., et al. (2015). Garlic and onions: their cancer prevention properties. *Cancer Prevention Research* (Philadelphia), 8(3), pp.181–89.

Fruit: low-sugar treats

Cordain, L. (n.d.) Fruits and sugars. The Paleo Diet, thepaleodiet.com/fruits-and-sugars.

Cordain, L., *The Paleo Diet: Lose weight and get healthy by eating the foods you were designed to eat* (John Wiley & Sons Ltd, revised edition, 2010).

Dairy: time to ditch it?

Animal Protection Institute. (2015). Dairy cows. Voiceless, voiceless.org.au/the-issues/dairy-cows.

Dairy Australia. (n.d.). Yield. Dairy Australia: Your Levy at Work, dairyaustralia.com.au/Markets-and-statistics/Production-and-sales/Milk/Yield.aspx.

Melnik, B. C. (2009). Milk – the promotor of chronic western diseases. *Medical Hypotheses*, 72(6), pp.631–39.

Grains: why we just don't need them

Davis, W. (2015). Top 10 reasons to kiss wheat and grains goodbye forever. Dr. William Davis: Cardiologist + Author + Health Crusader, 4 April, www.wheatbellyblog.com/2015/04/top-10-reasons-to-kiss-wheat-and-grains-goodbye-forever.

Davis, W., *Wheat Belly: The effortless health and weight-loss solution* (Harper Thorsons, 2015).

Pruimboom, L. and de Punder, K. (2015). The opioid effects of gluten exorphins: asymptomatic celiac disease. *Journal of Health, Population and Nutrition*, 33, 24.

Shun-Zi, J., et al. (2012). A study of circulating gliadin antibodies in schizophrenia among a Chinese population. *Schizophrenia Bulletin*, 38(3), pp.514–18.

Trivedi, M. S., et al. (2014). Food-derived opioid peptides inhibit cysteine uptake with redox and epigenetic consequences. *Journal of Nutritional Biochemistry*, 25(10), pp.1011–18.

The trouble with legumes

Bajaj, J. K. et al. (2016). Various possible toxicants involved in thyroid dysfunction: a review, *Journal of Clinical and Diagnostic Research*, 10(1), pp.FE01–03.

Freed, D. L. J. (1999). Do dietary lectins cause disease? *British Medical Journal*, 318(7190), pp.1023–24. Gedgaudas, N., *Primal Fat Burner: Live longer, slow aging, super-power your brain, and save your life with a high-fat, low-carb paleo die*t, Chapter 3, A is for agriculture and adapting to glucose' (Atria Books, 2017).

Mercola, J. (2012). Eating grains can 'tear holes' in your gut. Mercola, 21 January, articles.mercola.com/sites/articles/archive/2012/01/21/grains-causing-gut-leaks.aspx.

Nagel, R., (2010). Living with phytic acid. Weston A. Price Foundation, 26 March, www.westonaprice.org/health-topics/vegetarianism-and-plant-foods/living-with-phytic-acid.

Microbiome: trust your gut

Francescone, R., et al. (2014). Microbiome, inflammation and cancer. *Cancer Journal*, 20(3), pp.181–89.

Hill-Burns, E. M., et al. (2017). Parkinson's disease and Parkinson's disease medications have distinct signatures of the gut microbiome. *Movement Disorders*, 32(5), pp.739–49.

University of Alabama at Birmingham (2017). Link between microbiome in the gut, Parkinson's discovered. Science Daily, 2 March, www.sciencedaily.com/releases/2017/03/170302133859.htm.

Perlmutter, D., *Brain Maker: The power of gut microbes to heal and protect your brain – for life* (Yellow Kite, 2015).

Selhub, E. M., et al. (2014). Fermented foods, microbiota, and mental health: ancient practice meets nutritional psychiatry. *Journal of Physiological Anthropology*, 33, 2.

Sender, R., et al. (2016). Revised estimates for the number of human and bacteria cells in the body. *PLoS Biology*, 14(8), e1002533.

Vighi, G., et al. (2008). Allergy and the gastrointestinal system. Clinical and Experimental Immunology, 153 (Suppl.1), pp.3–6.

Fermented foods: boost your microbiome

Body Ecology. (n.d.). Why fermented foods may help reduce the toxic mercury in your body. Body Ecology, bodyecology.com/articles/fermented_foods_and_mercury.php.

Mueller, N. T., et al. (2015). The infant microbiome development: mom matters. *Trends in Molecular Medicine*, 21(2), 109–17.

Sandrine P., C., et al. (2016). The gut microbiota: a major player in the toxicity of environmental pollutants?. *npj Biofilms and Microbiomes*, 2, p.16003.

Probiotics and prebiotics: powerful game-changers

Cebeci, A., et al. (2003). Properties of potential probiotic *Lactobacillus plantarum* strains. *Food Microbiology*, 20(5), pp.511–18.

Dicks, L. M. and Botes, M. (2010). Probiotic lactic acid bacteria in the gastro-intestinal tract: health benefits, safety and mode of action. *Beneficial Microbes*, 1(1), pp.11–29.

Mercola, J. (2012). *Probiotics and Fermented Foods for a Healthy Immune System*. [online] Mercola.com. Available at: http://articles.mercola.com/sites/articles/archive/2012/07/14/gut-microbes-for-healthy-immune-system.aspx.

Niedzelin, K. et al. (2001). A controlled, double-blind, randomized study on the efficacy of *Lactobacillus plantarum* 299V in patients with irritable bowel syndrome. *European Journal of Gastroenterology and Hepatology*, 13(10), pp.1143–7.

Roberfroid, M.B. (2000). Prebiotics and probiotics: are they functional foods? *American Journal of Clinical Nutrition*, 71(6), pp.1682s–87s.

Slavin, J. (2013). Fibre and prebiotics: mechanisms and health benefits. *Nutrients*, 5(4), pp.1417–35.

Wasilewski, A. and Zielińska, M. (2015). Beneficial effects of probiotics, prebiotics, synbiotics, and psychobiotics in inflammatory bowel disease. *Inflammatory Bowel Diseases*, 21(7): pp.1674–82.

Bone broth: brewing the benefits

Daniel, K. (2003). Why broth is beautiful: essential roles for proline, glycine and gelatin. Weston A. Price Foundation, 18 June, www.westonaprice.org/health-topics/why-broth-is-beautiful-essential-roles-for-proline-glycine-and-gelatin.

Morell, S. F. (2000). Broth is beautiful. Weston A. Price Foundation, 1 January, www.westonaprice.org/health-topics/food-features/broth-is-beautiful.

Rennard, B. O., et al. (2000). Chicken soup inhibits neutrophil chemotaxis in vitro. *Chest*, 118(4), pp.1150–57.

Tannahill, R., *Food in History* (Broadway Books, revised edition,1995).

Wald. A. and Adibi, S. A. (1982). Stimulation of gastric acid secretion by glycine and related oligopeptides in humans. *American Journal of Physiology*, 242(2), pp. G85-G88.

Beverages: benefits and pitfalls

Fagherazzi, G., et al. (2013). Consumption of artificially and sugar-sweetened beverages and incident type 2 diabetes in the Étude Épidémiologique auprès des femmes de la Mutuelle Générale de l'Éducation Nationale–European Prospective Investigation into Cancer and Nutrition cohort. *American Journal of Clinical Nutrition*, 97(3), pp.517–23.

Keijzers, G. B., et al. (2002). Caffeine can decrease insulin sensitivity in humans. *Diabetes Care*, 25, pp.364–69.

Shell, E. R. (2015). Artificial sweeteners may change our gut bacteria in dangerous ways. 1 April, *Scientific American*, 18 June, www.scientificamerican.com/article/artificial-sweeteners-may-change-our-gut-bacteria-in-dangerous-ways.

Fasting: a beginner's guide

Collier, R. (2013). Intermittent fasting: the science of going without. *Canadian Medical Association Journal*, 185(9): E363–64.

Fung, J., *The Complete Guide to Fasting* (Victory Belt, 2016).

Fung, J., *The Obesity Code* (Scribe, 2016).

Gnanou, J. V., et al. (2015). Effects of Ramadan fasting on glucose homeostasis and adiponectin levels in healthy adult males. *Journal of Diabetes and Metabolic Disorders*, 2015; 14, 55.

Patterson, R. E., et al. (2015). Intermittent fasting and human metabolic health. *Journal of the Academy of Nutrition and Dietetics*, 115(8): 1203–1212.

Resting

Cappuccio F. P., et al. (2008). Meta-analysis of short sleep duration and obesity in children and adults. *Sleep*, 31(5), pp.619–26.

Ip, M. and Mokhlesi, B. (2007). Sleep and glucose intolerance/diabetes mellitus. *Sleep Medicine Clinics*, 2(1): 19–29.

van der Lely, S., et al. (2015). Blue blocker glasses as a countermeasure for alerting effects of evening light-emitting diode screen exposure in male teenagers. *Journal of Adolescent Health*, 56(1), pp.113–19.

Meditation

Askenasy, J. and Lehmann, J. (2013). Consciousness, brain, neuroplasticity. *Frontiers in Psychology*, 4, 412.

Laneri, D., et al. (2015). Effects of long-term mindfulness meditation on brain's white matter microstructure and its aging. *Frontiers in Aging Neuroscience*, 7, 254.

Young, S. N. (2011). Biologic effects of mindfulness meditation: growing insights into neurobiologic aspects of the prevention of depression. *Journal of Psychiatry and Neuroscience*, 36(2): 75–77.

Mindfulness

Lim, D., et al. (2015). Mindfulness and compassion: an examination of mechanism and scalability. *PloS ONE*, 10(2), e0118221.

THANKS

A mountain of gratitude to my glorious family, especially my wonderful wife, Nic, and my two amazing daughters, Indii and Chilli. You three angels are a constant source of pure inspiration and happiness, and it is indeed a humbling honour to walk beside you all throughout this life. Thank you for being your bright, fun-loving, authentic and unconditionally loving selves.

To the absolute wonder twins, Monica and Jacinta Cannataci, you both add your own magic essence to everything we create together, and this book just wouldn't be the same without your input. Thank you both for working so graciously and tirelessly, and for all that you do!

To the incredible photography and styling team of Steve Brown, Deb Kaloper, William Meppem, Rob Palmer, Mark Roper and Lucy Tweed, you all bring a unique sense of beauty that never ceases to be exceptionally pleasing in every way, and I'm endlessly thankful for you all.

To Ingrid Ohlsson and Mary Small, thank you for passionately orchestrating the path that allows so much goodness to come to life. It is a pleasure to work with you both, always!

Thanks to Clare Marshall, for making sure everything is as it should be. It is a joy to have you crossing the T's and dotting the I's.

To Charlotte Ree, thanks for being the best publicist any author could wish to work with.

To Alison Cowan and Megan Johnston, thank you for your careful and thorough editing.

To Emily O'Neill, thank you for creating such a gorgeous design for the book.

A very warm thank you to my sweet mum, Joy. Among many things, you passed on your love of cooking and there's no doubt that I wouldn't be here without you.

I also wish to express a huge thank you to my teachers, peers, mentors and friends, who are all genuinely working towards creating a healthier world and who are all in their own right true forces for good: Nora Gedgaudas and Lisa Collins, Trevor Hendy, Rudy Eckhardt, Dr Pete Bablis, Dr David Perlmutter, Dr Alessio Fasano, Dr Kelly Brogan, Dr William Davis, Dr Joseph Mercola, Helen Padarin, Dr Natasha Campbell-McBride, Dr Frank Lipman, Dr Libby, Prof. Tim Noakes, Pete Melov and Prof. Martha Herbert, to name a few.

INDEX

A PLUM BOOK

First published in 2017 by
Pan Macmillan Australia Pty Limited
Level 25, 1 Market Street,
Sydney, NSW 2000, Australia

Level 3, 112 Wellington Parade,
East Melbourne, VIC 3002, Australia

Design and illustrations by Emily O'Neill
Edited by Alison Cowan and Megan Johnston
Index by Jo Rudd
Photography by William Meppem (with additional photography
by Steve Brown, Armelle Habib. Rob Palmer and Mark Roper)
Prop and food styling by Deborah Kaloper and Lucy Tweed
Food preparation by Jacinta and Monica Cannatacci
Typeset by Emily O'Neill
Colour reproduction by Splitting Image Colour Studio
Printed and bound in China by 1010 Printing International Limited

A CIP catalogue record for this book is available
from the National Library of Australia.

10 9 8 7 6 5 4 3 2 1